AGING IN WORLD HISTORY

In *Aging in World History*, David G. Troyansky presents the first global history of aging. At a time when demographic aging has become a source of worldwide concern and more people are reaching an advanced age than ever before, coming to terms with the history of old age informs the discourse of aging in the modern world. This concise volume expands that history beyond the West to show how attitudes toward aging, the experiences of the aged, and relevant demographic patterns have varied and coalesced over time and across the world.

From the ancient world to the present, this book introduces students and general readers to the history of aging on two levels: the experience of individual men and women, and the transformation of populations. With its attention to cultural traditions, medicalization, decades of historical scholarship, and current gerontology, *Aging in World History* is the perfect starting point for an exploration of this increasingly universal aspect of human experience.

David G. Troyansky is Professor of History at Brooklyn College and the Graduate Center, City University of New York

THEMES IN WORLD HISTORY

Series editor: Peter N. Stearns

The *Themes in World History* series offers focused treatment of a range of human experiences and institutions in the world history context. The purpose is to provide serious, if brief, discussions of important topics as additions to textbook coverage and document collections. The treatments will allow students to probe particular facets of the human story in greater depth than textbook coverage allows, and to gain a fuller sense of historians' analytical methods and debates in the process. Each topic is handled over time – allowing discussions of changes and continuities. Each topic is assessed in terms of a range of different societies and religions – allowing comparisons of relevant similarities and differences. Each book in the series helps readers deal with world history in action, evaluating global contexts as they work through some of the key components of human society and human life.

Gender in World History
Peter N. Stearns

Consumerism in World History: The Global Transformation of Desire
Peter N. Stearns

Warfare in World History
Michael S. Neiberg

Disease and Medicine in World History
Sheldon Watts

Western Civilization in World History
Peter N. Stearns

The Indian Ocean in World History
Milo Kearney

Asian Democracy in World History
Alan T. Wood

Revolutions in World History
Michael D. Richards

Migration in World History
Patrick Manning

Sports in World History
David G. McComb

The United States in World History
Edward J. Davies, II

Food in World History
Jeffrey M. Pilcher

Childhood in World History
Peter N. Stearns

Religion in World History
John Super and Briane Turley

Poverty in World History
Steven M Beaudoin

Premodern Travel in World History
Steven S. Gosch and Peter N. Stearns

Premodern Trade in World History
Richard L. Smith

Sexuality in World History
Peter N. Stearns

Globalization in World History
Peter N. Stearns

Jews and Judaism in World History
Howard N. Lupovitch

The Environment in World History
Stephen Mosley

Agriculture in World History
Mark B. Tauger

Science in World History
James Trefil

Alcohol in World History
Gina Hames

Human Rights in World History
Peter N. Stearns

Peace in World History
Peter N. Stearns

The Atlantic Slave Trade in World History
Jeremy Black

Aging in World History
David G. Troyansky

AGING IN WORLD HISTORY

David G. Troyansky

NEW YORK AND LONDON

First published 2016
by Routledge
711 Third Avenue, New York, NY 10017

and by Routledge
2 Park Square, Milton Park, Abingdon, Oxon OX14 4RN

Routledge is an imprint of the Taylor & Francis Group, an informa business

© 2016 David G. Troyansky

The right of David G. Troyansky to be identified as author of this work has been asserted by him in accordance with sections 77 and 78 of the Copyright, Designs and Patents Act 1988.

All rights reserved. No part of this book may be reprinted or reproduced or utilised in any form or by any electronic, mechanical, or other means, now known or hereafter invented, including photocopying and recording, or in any information storage or retrieval system, without permission in writing from the publishers.

Trademark notice: Product or corporate names may be trademarks or registered trademarks, and are used only for identification and explanation without intent to infringe.

Library of Congress Cataloging in Publication Data
Troyansky, David G.
Aging in world history / David G. Troyansky.
pages cm. — (Themes in world history)
Includes index.
1. Aging—History. 2. Older people—History. 3. Population aging—History.
I. Title.
HQ1061.T78 2015
305.26—dc23
2015012868

ISBN: 978-0-415-77906-7 (hbk)
ISBN: 978-0-415-77907-4 (pbk)
ISBN: 978-1-315-67518-3 (ebk)

Typeset in Bembo
by Taylor & Francis Books

For my father...
...et pour Françoise Cribier

CONTENTS

Acknowledgements	xi
Preface	xiii

SECTION I
Theoretical Concerns, "Natural" Aging, and Classical Prescriptions and Representations — 1

1 Introduction: Historians Look at Aging and the Aged — 3

2 Aging among Hunters and Gatherers, Agriculturalists, and Early City Dwellers — 9

3 Old Age in Classical Civilizations: From Asia to the Near East and Mediterranean — 16

SECTION II
Medieval to Early Modern Transformations — 37

4 Aging in the Middle Ages and the Renaissance — 39

5 Early Modern Aging and the Aged in Europe and North America — 57

SECTION III
Transitions to Modernity   65

  6 Cultural Transitions and Implications for the Aged   67

  7 Demographic Transitions and Implications for the Aged   74

SECTION IV
Modernity and Old Age   79

  8 Framing the Old Person as Pensioner and Old Age as a Social Problem in the Nineteenth and Early Twentieth Centuries   81

  9 Old Age in the Context of Colonialism, Imperialism, and Decolonization   87

 10 Aging and the Welfare State   96

SECTION V
Globalizing, Medicalizing, and Disciplining Old Age   105

 11 Aging in a Global Context   107

 12 Aging, Medicalization, and the Discipline of Gerontology   116

 13 Aging in Present and Future   127

Index   147

ACKNOWLEDGEMENTS

Every book takes time. This one took longer than expected. Peter Stearns asked me several times to write it. Eventually, I agreed. Stephen Gosch, Joel Rosenthal, and Pat Thane reviewed the proposal and offered thoughtful and helpful suggestions that gave me the courage to overcome my residual resistance. The existing scholarship on the history of aging and the aged is very Western, and this book is part of a series in world history. It has required me to learn about places that are far from my usual scholarly concerns. For that I'm grateful. Even though I am now turning back to a topic in French history, my approach will forever be more "global." The delay was also the result of having taken on administrative responsibilities for longer than expected. Happily, a sabbatical from Brooklyn College allowed me to finish. I thank Chairperson Chris Ebert, Provost Bill Tramontano, fellow Francophone scholar President Karen Gould, and the department staff, Arline Neftleberg, Anne Ciarlo, and Lorraine Greenfield. Thanks to the Tow Professorship for important financial assistance. Dean Kimberley Phillips and I shared thoughts on balancing scholarship and administration (and much else), and Interim Dean Matthew Moore provided support and friendship over dinners and chamber music. I wouldn't have gotten through all that administrative work if not for the guidance of fellow chairs, who, like my inspiring students, really are too numerous to name. Kyle Francis, who has launched his own career as a historian, provided bibliographical assistance at the Graduate Center of CUNY. He and current student Megan Brown provided help at an important time. At the last minute, Helen Georgas of the Brooklyn College Library made a crucial purchase and old friend and colleague Robert Aldrich sent news of a new publication before boarding a plane in Bangkok. The editorial team at Routledge was very kind about adjusting the schedule of delivery. Thanks to Kimberly Guinta and her predecessors. When I finally submitted a draft, Peter Stearns took about a day to send suggestions for revision. They were important, and they were feasible, as were the recommendations on the next draft. We should all have such editors.

In retrospect, I had been preparing to write this book for longer than I was aware. After publishing on old age in eighteenth-century France, I was asked to write pieces in collective works on old age over longer periods of time and vaster geographic spaces. Thanks to Tom Cole, John Merriman, Susannah Ottaway, and Pat Thane. Things were also percolating through conversations with Tim Alborn, Jean-Pierre Bardet, Aline Charles, Françoise Cribier, Christoph Conrad, Elise Feller, Vincent Gourdon, and others. Françoise has been my long-term guide to European gerontology, a model practitioner of multidisciplinary social science, and, with the late Daniel, a great friend and host. For a few years, Robert Binstock would send me books to review for *The Gerontologist*. They included volumes on ancient Rome, American retirement, and much else. Over the years, I had evidently been thinking beyond the boundaries of my own training and early experience. So I took the plunge into world history. For help, I turned to Swapna Banerjee, Bilal Ibrahim, Andrew Meyer, Kavita Sivaramakrishnan, and Megan Vaughan. Thanks, all. And thanks, Megan, Kavita, and Andy, for reading at very short notice. All of the above have taught me much, but I remain responsible for any errors that have crept into the work.

Finally, I thank my family. Amy, you have put up with this project for as long as I have. It was a part of our lives in Brooklyn, at Lost Farm (thanks, Will; thanks, Ole), and in Paris (thanks, Sophie; thanks, Scott). I can't say that you always believed it would be finished, but we do share in the joy that it is. I won't say more because you believe that private lives should remain private. Anna, you have enriched our lives in these last months in Paris and given us great hope for the future. Aaron, you are our wonderful link to the non-academic world, but thanks for chasing down a last-minute citation. My father, Howard Troyansky, has provided a model of successful aging and extraordinarily important emotional support over a difficult period of time. My mother, Leila Troyansky, didn't live to see me begin the project; more tragically, my sister Valerie didn't live to see its end.

Paris, February 2015

PREFACE

Contemporary concerns about aging societies have stimulated interest in past ways of growing old. Historians have investigated the experience of the aged, cultural representations of old age, and the phenomenon of demographic aging. In some cases they begin with the observation that collectively we are experiencing what the late Peter Laslett called a "fresh map of life," one in which the vast majority of the human population can live out a life course that was experienced by a much smaller segment of the population in the past. Yet, some always did live into what they named (and we would recognize) as old age. Their experience has become the norm. It's not that we have transformed the species; rather, more of us experience what was previously permitted only a few. In one sense, this represents a great triumph of life over death. In another, it may mean an unprecedented challenge. Old age may bring honor and prestige, but it also may bring physical and cognitive decline and intergenerational conflict over resources.

That duality meant that the historians who pioneered the study of old age in the 1970s and 1980s often found themselves dealing with two very different master narratives. One was a story of progress in which life expectancy at birth increased from the 20s and 30s to the 60s, 70s, and 80s. Most of that improvement took place in the twentieth century, so tellers of the progressive tale sometimes expended little energy looking before the late nineteenth century. Those who focused on stages of life and especially the transition from work to retirement emphasized the last two centuries; yet, some looked for precursors and delved back before 1800. Still others, especially those interested in cultural representations of older people, found that there were important transitions that predated even the eighteenth century. And many key cultural representations involved continuity going back to the ancient world.

The other master narrative was one of decline. And it was a narrative that itself has a long history. When I began a study of aging and the aged in eighteenth-century France, I cited an early nineteenth-century lament about how the aged no longer received the respect they were traditionally accorded. One can move deep into the past and find similar sentiments. Eventually, it occurred to historians looking at early modern, medieval, and ancient eras that it made little sense to speak of one-directional evolution or one big change.

Falling into the trap of seeing only one change was very easy. As human beings, the species imbued with a sophisticated historical memory, we may be tempted to contrast present with past, how things are with how things were. This may happen in political rhetoric, classrooms, and families. The narrative of decline, involving a large dose of nostalgia, is found in many of our cultural inheritances, even if, especially in the USA, it is opposed by a rhetoric of improvement from one generation to the next. And in the 1970s, when historians looked to other disciplines, they found that sociologists and gerontologists (practitioners of a field whose history is only beginning to be appreciated and written) were operating within a very dualistic universe. "Modernization" was said to have harmed the position of the aged. The very thin anthropological and historical literature hadn't yet offered enough evidence to challenge that story. But eventually, historians and anthropologists did the research that filled out the record, and sociologists in some cases stepped back from a presentist view of the world to appreciate the complicated histories that informed people's lives. Appreciation of the role of social security systems and of medical progress may even have led to a new version of the progressive narrative. Never were the aged so many, and never did they have it so good. But as more and more studies appeared, the record seemed increasingly mixed and complicated. And a deeper look at representations, interpretations, and prescriptions related to growing old revealed that our cultural inheritances transcended simple narratives of progress or decline, and they provided materials with which people could construct their own versions of late life.

A challenge to anyone trying to survey the literature on the world history of aging and the aged is that that literature, mostly tied to national histories, has been overwhelmingly Western. Here and there we find studies in other parts of the world, particularly Asia, but attempts to conceptualize a history of aging have generally left out much of the globe.

Peter Stearns made that clear 20 years ago. Since then, the appearance of a more international literature has allowed some rethinking. This book represents one attempt to reach for a more global context. It is the work of an American specialist in European (particularly French) history who sees the project as an exploratory exercise, an opportunity to review a world-wide literature and move beyond received wisdom about attitudes and experiences running from the ancient world to the present.

The book seeks to introduce history and gerontology students as well as general readers to historical ways of thinking about aging in two senses: the experience of individuals and the transformation of populations. The former is something we can study over long stretches of time and throughout the world. How long did people live? What could they have expected in their later years? How did they represent old age, and how did representation and experience vary by gender and class? Major studies already exist on such topics in ancient, medieval, and modern history; thus, there are opportunities for comparative historical insights. The latter (demographic aging) concerns the modern period, in which people throughout the world, having had very different historical experiences, have come to face similar challenges with comparable expectations. How do people balance expectations of decline and healthy retirement? Is a medicalized old age a global phenomenon? Do traditional representations of the elderly continue to shape people's understandings of their earthly fate? The book surveys an innovative historical literature and provides opportunities for examining how a contemporary "problem" looked in the past and how traditional experience and wisdom survive and function.

The global reach of the book, divided into five parts, is most apparent in the first, third, fourth, and fifth sections; the second section focuses on the West for two major reasons. First, the historical literature on old age from late antiquity through the early modern period almost completely neglects the rest of the world. This makes it exceedingly difficult to write a global survey of the era. Second, the long period encompassing the Middle Ages, the Renaissance and Reformation, and the early modern period prepared the way for the modern imposition of Western models on the wider world. The spread of both Christianity and secularism, the rise of European states, and the reach of Western science and capitalism all had a profound long-term impact on the rest of the world. Nonetheless, even the chapters in this section will provide some glimpses of that wider world, whether through representations of the aged in Islamic cultures, scientific and medical thought in Asia, or the question of retirement from state service.

The first section introduces theoretical concerns, understandings of "natural" or "traditional" ways of growing old, and diverse cultural prescriptions and representations. The book begins (chapter 1) with observations of contemporary interest in both old age and demographic aging, the variety of approaches taken by historians, and attempts to create a long-term chronology. It moves (chapter 2) to what we might know, from rather sketchy evidence, of aging among hunters and gatherers, agriculturalists, and the earliest city dwellers. It then explores (chapter 3) old age as a theme in classical civilizations from India and China to the Near East and the Mediterranean. In each of those cases, it discusses aging and the aged in their particular historical settings and as background to their more modern cultural heirs.

The second section covers key issues, primarily in the West, from the medieval to the early modern era. It includes a chapter (chapter 4) on medieval and Renaissance Europe, accompanied by brief looks at the Islamic world and Japan, with emphasis on religious and secular ways of understanding old age, and one (chapter 5) on the early modern era in Europe and North America, with attention to the role of the state and the origins of modern social thought concerning old age.

A third section explores transitions to modernity. Chapter 6 covers changes in the way old people were represented in the West. Chapter 7 covers the demographic transitions and their implications for the aged worldwide. Readers may consider the relative importance of cultural and demographic changes that led to the modern world.

A fourth section looks at phenomena that we associate with modernity. Chapter 8 focuses on social conditions in the nineteenth and twentieth centuries, as populations are viewed in terms of youth and age, and old age, particularly when viewed in terms of gender and class differences, becomes framed as a social problem. Discussion of the role of aging in the relative strength of nations provides a transition to an exploration (chapter 9) of old age in the context of colonialism, imperialism, and decolonization. Pensions and retirement are the keys in chapter 10, which recounts the history of social security systems and welfare states and focuses on Europe and North America, Australia and New Zealand, and Japan.

The final section explores the contemporary world. Chapter 11 focuses on economically poorer settings, using African and Middle Eastern examples, India, and China, as well as the former communist nations that experienced rapid transformation affecting the aged. There the book considers the impact of demography and population programs as well as the survival of the kinds of cultural representations evoked earlier in the book. Returning to primarily Western developments that have had global consequences, chapter 12 explores the medicalization of old age and the emergence of a discipline of gerontology. Chapter 13 examines how current tendencies in gerontology present aging and the aged throughout the world and how the subject of old age reaches a broad public, but it does not ignore how individual populations sometimes resist "expert" views and how individual elders affirm their own agency and subjectivity. Readers are invited to think about the relationships between past, present, and future.

Works Cited and Further Reading

Peter Laslett, *A Fresh Map of Life: The Emergence of the Third Age*, second edition (London: Palgrave Macmillan, 1996); first edition (London: Weidenfeld and Nicolson, 1989). David G. Troyansky, *Old Age in the Old Regime: Image and Experience in Eighteenth-Century France* (Ithaca: Cornell University Press, 1989). For the classic statement on aging and modernization, see Donald O. Cowgill and Lowell D. Holmes, eds., *Aging and Modernization* (NY: Appleton-Century-Crofts, 1972). For the challenge of writing a world history of aging, see Peter N. Stearns, "Elders in World History," chapter 16 in *Handbook of the Humanities and Aging*, edited by Thomas R. Cole, David D. Van Tassel, and Robert Kastenbaum (NY: Springer, 1992).

SECTION I

Theoretical Concerns, "Natural" Aging, and Classical Prescriptions and Representations

1

INTRODUCTION: HISTORIANS LOOK AT AGING AND THE AGED

Thirty years ago a first wave of scholarly publications on the history of old age emerged, building upon multiple concerns of the era. Among them were the phenomenon of demographic aging, an awareness of cultural change in the post-industrial world, and public policy debates related to retirement and social security systems. Associated with them were challenges having to do with work and leisure, grandparenthood, medicine, and politics.

Early histories of aging and the aged took a number of approaches. Some focused on demographic aging and perceived demographic challenge. Others looked at how the evolution of the life course was related to changes in workplace, family, and leisure activities. Still others focused on cultural representations. A few paid more than cursory attention to socio-economic and gender differences. A quick overview will present those approaches and related attempts to create a long-term chronology.

One obvious source of concern was demographic aging, something that had been identified decades earlier by some of the pioneers of historical demography but largely left aside while issues of fertility, mortality, and migration took precedence. The increasing share of over-60s in populations represented a challenge. The initial cause of the phenomenon was falling fertility—aging cohorts were growing as younger cohorts were shrinking—but eventually higher survival rates in advanced age played a significant role. Historical demography provided the language for understanding these phenomena, but interpretations varied, from fears of national decline vis-à vis younger populations in rival countries to celebratory descriptions of triumphs over death.

Early demographic studies, evoking gendered responsibilities for falling rates of birth, often included political language about decline. More recent demographic literature has sometimes freed itself of that political content and offered a more

4   Theoretical Concerns

balanced and nuanced interpretation, but even the seemingly neutral presentation of numbers requires some interpretation.

Another source of concern derived from changes in the modern and postmodern life course. Social history provided the main approach and the obvious chronology. Although sociologists and historians were already casting doubt on "modernization theory," the idea of a transformation from traditional to modern held on in the earliest histories of old age. Traditional authority vs. the modern demeaning of the aged was a primary theme. Nonetheless, some historians turned that scheme upside down and suggested that it was in the modern world of social security that elders saw their situations improve. Thus, for some it was about improvement, for others decline. Either way, it was a simple story.

British historian Peter Laslett was probably most outspoken about the novelty of aged populations, and his writings and other professional activities represented a conscious remaking of his own career. He had begun as a specialist in the history of political philosophy and culture, but he was best known for his work in family history, household reconstitution, and the quantitative and comparative studies of early modern and modern populations undertaken by the Cambridge Group for the History of Population and Social Structure. His name is immortalized beyond his own work in the typology of household structures (Laslett types), and that early family history included references to the family lives of the aged, whether as members of extended households, nuclear families, or solitaries. A generation of historians explored household structures as they evolved from one type to another. Central to this approach was the question of who resided with whom as well as the usual demographer's questions of birth, marriage, and death rates. A difficult but essential question was that of the older person's authority. Was it maintained? If so, how? If not, what was the resulting plight of the elder?

Later in his career, Laslett "discovered" old age and went beyond scholarly practice by involving populations of retired persons in intellectual life through universities of the third age in Great Britain. Thus, for historians of aging and the aged, he was a figure who looked at social structure, focused on the transformation of populations, and began to think about how older people might engage in the life of the mind after their active careers had ended. That practical work was matched by others' in the elderhostel system in North America. But the scholarly initiative was something that built upon strengths in social history, a desire for comparative quantitative study, and something of the prophet's single-mindedness. He wrote of a "fresh map of life" for which individuals, nations, and NGOs needed to prepare. We will return to those themes throughout this book, but it should be mentioned that Laslett's focus on "age-transformed" populations as unprecedented meant a down-grading of studies that explored eras before that transformation, and that was an oversight.

Some of the early histories of old age that posited a major shift in the status of the aged found evidence of change in periods that predated the large demographic shift that so animated Laslett. The first American histories of old age told stories of decline in status but dated the shift differently. David Hackett Fischer's *Growing Old in America* found it in the Revolutionary and early republican era. Andrew Achenbaum found it somewhat later, as did Brian Gratton and Carole Haber. Fischer was strong on republican political culture and questions of authority, Achenbaum, who would later write on social security and the history of gerontology, at first stuck to matters generally associated with the construction of a nation at a time of "modernization," and Gratton and Haber addressed issues of the state and medicine. Despite their creative use of sources and often subtle appreciation of historical change, they often spoke of tradition and modernity. On the side of tradition were patriarchal power, tension between generations over household authority, and a relatively small percentage of people over the age of 60. On the side of modernity were industry, urbanization, higher literacy, and an increasing percentage of older people.

In European history, that traditional/modern or preindustrial/industrial divide characterized some major publications. Peter Stearns explored medical and scientific components to modernizing old age in looking at nineteenth- and twentieth-century France (*Old Age in European Society*), and his edited volume on preindustrial old age extended the boundaries beyond the Western world (*Old Age in Preindustrial Society*, 1982). It also called for greater complexity ("a richer texture") in thinking about historical change: "A final balance sheet on preindustrial old age and its qualities compared with those of the modern counterpart must surely take into account a variety of plusses and minuses, not the simplest kind of good/bad contrast" (10–11).

Publications from the late 1990s and early 2000s offer a sense of where the field was evolving. Paul Johnson and Pat Thane's *Old Age from Antiquity to Post-Modernity* (1998) offered studies from ancient to contemporary worlds and identified three major issues for historians of old age: participation, well-being, and status. Susannah Ottaway, L.A. Botelho, and Katharine Kittredge, in *Power and Poverty: Old Age in the Pre-Industrial Past* (2002), returned to the period covered by Stearns' collection, but its key words are authority, autonomy, and responsibility. In both the 1998 and 2002 collections, the key themes were social historical in nature, but some contributors allowed exploration of people's subjectivities. Ottaway and Botelho's own monographs on early modern England did the same.

It had dawned on historians that the story was more one of ambiguity. Like gerontologists, they took a lesson from the world of anthropology and made a more cultural turn. My own book on eighteenth-century France displays characteristics of that earlier mode of traditional/modern but also points in the direction of cultural representations as playing a significant role in the history of old age. It posited a cultural shift from a religious world to one of Enlightenment, characterized by a revival of certain classical themes. And it juxtaposed that cultural history with social historical trends.

The literature on American history also demonstrated a cultural turn. Most influential was probably Thomas Cole's *The Journey of Life: A Cultural History of*

Aging in America. It took seriously the religious and artistic representations of old age in America, particularly in the nineteenth century, and it suggested that Americans in the twentieth and twenty-first centuries were struggling with the problem of hanging onto some sort of meaning of late life.

Still to come was the study of the aging self and the significance of gender. Howard Chudacoff examined age consciousness in the United States. Terri L. Premo and Lois Banner pioneered the study of older women in the United States and elsewhere, Lynn Botelho and Pat Thane produced an edited volume on aging women in early modern and modern England, and Elise Feller, while saying much about social class in the construction of the category of the old in her book on France in the first half of the twentieth century, argued for the importance of gender. Men and women had different experiences of aging, and women were becoming an increasing majority of the aged in the twentieth century, but some research revealed ways in which the sexes were growing more alike. Generalization was difficult. W. Andrew Achenbaum and Jill Quadagno focused attention on aging and social security, and Vincent Gourdon produced the first major historical study of grandparenthood. As in so many areas of historical research, we gained in depth of understanding of particular historical settings even as we may have lost touch with grand narratives. The chapters that follow will report findings in those specialized studies, and they will move chronologically from antiquity to the present. But before we move to the historical universe, let us look at the anthropological world. For just as historians were attempting to make sense of aging and the aged, so too anthropologists were looking afresh at something that was right in front of their eyes when they depended so often on elderly informants.

Works Cited and Further Reading

Early works on the history of old age include Keith Thomas, *Age and Authority in Early Modern England* (London: British Academy, 1976); John Demos's essay on old age reprinted in *Past, Present, and Personal: The Family and the Life Course in American History* (NY: Oxford University Press, 1986); and Peter N. Stearns, *Old Age in European Society: The Case of France* (NY: Holmes and Meier, 1976). Historians made important contributions to a couple of interdisciplinary volumes: Stuart F. Spicker, Kathleen M. Woodward, and David D. Van Tassel, eds., *Aging and the Elderly: Humanistic Perspectives in Gerontology* (Atlantic Highlands, N.J., Humanities Press, 1978), and David D. Van Tassel, ed., *Aging, Death, and the Completion of Being* (Philadelphia: University of Pennsylvania Press, 1979). A history of early modern aging in Germany is Peter Borscheid, *Geschichte des Alters, 16. Bis 18. Jahrhundert* (Münster: F. Coppenrath, 1987). An ambitious survey that has been taken to task for overgeneralizing is Georges Minois, *Histoire de la vieillesse: De l'antiquité à la Renaissance* (Paris: Fayard, 1987), English translation: *History of Old Age: From Antiquity to the Renaissance* (Chicago: University of Chicago Press, 1989); the follow-up volume by Jean-Pierre Bois, *Les vieux: de Montaigne aux premières retraites* (Paris: Fayard, 1989), which is generally more judicious, hasn't been translated. Some of the early histories of American aging include David Hackett Fischer, *Growing Old in America* (NY: Oxford University Press, 1977); Brian Gratton, *Urban Elders: Family, Work, and Welfare among Boston's Aged, 1890–1950* (Philadelphia: Temple University Press, 1985) which has much to say about the impact of Social Security; and Carole Haber, *Beyond Sixty-Five: The Dilemma of Old Age in America's Past* (NY: Cambridge University Press, 1983), which gives one of the best accounts of the role of medicine in the history of old age. A sociologist's attempt to test the "modernization" hypothesis in English history is Jill Quadagno, *Aging in Early Industrial Society: Work, Family, and Social Policy in Nineteenth Century England* (NY: Academic Press, 1982). In more recent times, the most successful one-volume treatment of aging in a national context is Pat Thane, *Old Age in English History: Past Experiences, Present Issues* (Oxford: Oxford University Press, 2000), and her richly illustrated edited book, *The Long History of Old Age* (London: Thames and Hudson, 2005), is a good place to start for aging in the Western world.

For the early demographic literature on aging, see Alfred Sauvy, whose posthumous *La vieillesse des nations* (Paris: Gallimard, 2001) was edited by Jean-Claude Chesnais; for a critical look at that literature and an original way of treating the history of aging in the modern period, see Patrice Bourdelais, *L'âge de la vieillesse* (Paris: Odile Jacob, 1993). For a more recent demographic overview, see Peter Uhlenberg, ed., *International Handbook of Population Aging* (Dordrecht: Springer, 2009).

Among the works of Peter Laslett and the Cambridge Group, see Laslett and Richard Wall, eds., *Household and Family in Past Time* (Cambridge: Cambridge University Press, 1972); Laslett, *Family Life and Illicit Love in Earlier Generations* (Cambridge: Cambridge University Press, 1977); Laslett, Richard Wall, and Jean Robin, eds., *Family Forms in Historic Europe* (Cambridge: Cambridge University Press, 1983). Growing out of that tradition but at times revealing Laslett's contemporary emphasis is David I. Kertzer and Peter Laslett, eds., *Aging in the Past: Demography, Society, and Old Age* (Berkeley: University of California Press, 1995).

W. Andrew Achenbaum, *Old Age in the New Land: The American Experience since 1790* (Baltimore: The Johns Hopkins University Press, 1978); Peter N. Stearns, ed., *Old Age in Preindustrial Society* (NY: Holmes and Meier, 1982); Paul Johnson and Pat Thane, eds., *Old Age from Antiquity to Post-Modernity* (London: Routledge, 1998); Susannah Ottaway, L.A. Botelho, and Katharine Kittredge, eds., *Power and Poverty: Old Age in the Pre-Industrial Past* (NY: Greenwood Press, 2002); Susannah Ottaway, *The Decline of Life: Old Age in Eighteenth-Century England* (Cambridge: Cambridge University Press, 2004); Lynn Botelho, *Old Age and the English Poor Law, 1500–1700* (Woodbridge: Boydell and Brewer, 2004); Thomas Cole, *The Journey of Life: A Cultural History of Aging in America* (NY: Cambridge University Press, 1992); Howard Chudacoff, *How Old Are You? Age Consciousness in American Culture* (Princeton: Princeton University Press, 1989); Terri L. Premo, *Winter*

Friends: Women Growing Old in the New Republic (Urbana: University of Illinois Press, 1990); Lois Banner, *In Full Flower: Aging Women, Power, and Sexuality* (NY: Knopf, 1992); Lynn Botelho and Pat Thane, eds., *Women and Ageing in Britain since 1500* (London: Addison Wesley Longmans, 2000); Elise Feller, *Histoire de la vieillesse en France, 1900–1950* (Paris: Seli Arslan, 2005); W. Andrew Achenbaum, *Shades of Gray: Old Age, American Values and Federal Policies since 1920* (Boston: Little Brown, 1983), and *Social Security: Visions and Revisions* (New York: Cambridge University Press, 1986); Jill Quadagno, *The Transformation of Old Age Security: Class and Politics in the American Welfare State* (Chicago: University of Chicago Press, 1988); Vincent Gourdon, *Histoire des grands-parents* (Paris: Perrin, 2001).

2

AGING AMONG HUNTERS AND GATHERERS, AGRICULTURALISTS, AND EARLY CITY DWELLERS

Anthropology's approach to old age parallels history's in that both disciplines saw important publications in the late 1970s and 1980s and a modest but steady stream of monographs ever since. The disciplines intersect in interesting ways, as they both are often concerned with matters of kinship, authority, and community, but the fundamental distinction that became somewhat blurred over time was between anthropological study of "primitive," relatively egalitarian, preliterate communities on the one hand and historical (and sociological) study of urbanized, industrialized, literate societies on the other. One of the important twentieth-century philosophical treatments of old age, *La vieillesse* by Simone de Beauvoir, presented the anthropological literature as presenting "natural" aging, the benchmark against which to measure "historical" societies. She found some mentions of the aged in a few ethnographic studies, but the most massive body of data concerning the aged in so-called "primitive" societies had been drawn from Human Relations Area Files and the 1945 volume by Leo Simmons *The Role of the Aged in Primitive Society*.

Simmons examined the status and treatment of the aged through various traits identified in 71 tribes around the world. He claimed that in the rudest of environments tribes were most generous in sharing food with the aged. As hunting and gathering gave way to herding and agriculture, communal sharing of food with the elderly often went into decline (Simmons, p. 35). But continued control of property rights provided a way in which the aged could secure their position. He distinguished between women's greater rights in "simple societies characterized by collection, hunting, and fishing, and also within the matrilineal type of family organization" and aged men's "greatest advantage in the control of property among farmers, and especially herders, as well as within the patriarchal system of family organizations and amid social traits characteristic of more advanced cultures" (p. 49).

Simmons found considerable, but not universal, prestige "accorded to the aged in primitive societies, but only under culturally determined circumstances and for a limited age period which rarely extended into decrepitude" (p. 81). The most fortunate of them could take on new economic, political, and cultural roles. Experience mattered in the exercise of rituals and ceremonies. Simmons' description of the elderly as repositories of knowledge is worth quoting at length:

> They have been esteemed as experts in solving the problems of life. They have supervised and instructed in the arts and crafts; and have initiated hazardous and important undertakings, such as house-building, boat construction, the planting and harvesting of crops, and warfare. They have been in constant demand for treating diseases, exorcising spirits, working charms, controlling the weather, conjuring enemies, and predicting the future. They have been accredited officiators in the great events of life, such as childbirth, child-naming, initiations, weddings, funerals, and the 'laying of ghosts.' They have also functioned frequently as leaders at social gatherings, and as directors of games, songs, dances, and festivals. In fact, hardly any of the great and critical occasions of life have not been presided over and supervised by some aged men and women. Truly have they been the guardians of life's emergencies, the custodians of knowledge, and the directors of ceremonies and pastimes. In possession of such great influence, they have been the chief conservators of the status quo. And finally, after death, they have become supernatural agents themselves, still expert in the tried and tested wisdom of the ages, and very jealous of any young upstarts who might presume to challenge or change the ancient folkways.
>
> *(pp. 175–176)*

With Simmons one risks overgeneralizing, but he still offers a place to start, a useful form of analysis, and themes that have been taken up by generations of anthropologists. They continue to see a major role for elders and even forms of gerontocracy among "simple" societies (Flanagan). The Samburu of northern Kenya are one example. Paul Spencer describes an age-grade system in which young men (the *moran*) form a set and are subordinated to their elders, but the young men put up with the system in anticipation that they will one day be elders themselves. The Mekranoti of central Brazil are another example, and Dennis Werner emphasizes the importance of ceremonial knowledge. But even among more complex societies, anthropologists emphasize the relationship between knowledge and power in which elders control forms of knowledge, maintain a connection to the spiritual, and play an important role in socializing the young. Sometimes older women play those roles, but it should be recognized that if inequality between old and young is mitigated by the idea that the young will eventually advance, inequality between the sexes remains.

There is, of course, a danger in attempting to generalize from individual cases of hunter-gatherers. The authors of a large study of demography and ecology in the world of a foraging forest people in Paraguay, the Ache, warn of that danger by pointing out great differences between groups. The Dobe !Kung of Botswana in southern Africa, for example, are characterized by low fertility and low mortality from violence. The Ache, by contrast, are characterized by high fertility and high mortality from violence. Yet, descriptions of Ache old age may well reflect patterns among some others. Older women were reported to continue collecting food and engaging in housework until around 60 and then to babysit grandchildren. Older men faced a transition when they could no longer hunt. At that point they foraged, made tools, and eventually babysat. But when men or women became too old to keep up with the band, they were abandoned or killed. In the time of this particular study, only old women were killed by band members, "hit over the head with an ax when they were not looking" (Hill and Hurtado, p. 236). Such "senilicide" was not common among others. The Inuit supposedly engaged in it, but the !Kung did not. Nevertheless, the !Kung elderly didn't seem to live much into a period of dependence, which followed a stage anthropologists described as one of "retirement" (Howell, pp. 41–43).

Physical anthropologists have explored bones and fossils and even made comparative studies of aging among different primates. They emphasize the shape of the human life course as being fairly constant, with a long period of dependency, a relatively long period of menopause, and an important role for grandparents (Gurven and Kaplan). Specialists in prehistory suggest that first predators and then warfare kept population in check but that eventually "at a very early date in the history of mankind mechanisms based on custom or culture were established in order to control fertility and thereby maintain the rate of population growth at around zero" (Masset, p. 79). Preferred methods may have included taboos on sexual behavior, control of marriage, or infanticide, but here we are in the realm of speculation. And we are far from the modern era in which control of fertility would lead to demographic aging. Physical evidence suggests that less than half of those who reached the age of 20 would also reach 60. The implication is that the fewer the elders the greater the honor they enjoyed. Yet, scientists see a common human pattern of increases of mortality at 40 and modal age of death just past 70 for hunter-gatherers (Gurven and Kaplan, pp. 348–349). Moreover, paleoanthropologist Rachel Caspari has found evidence of a shift around 30,000 years ago in the fossil record of human adults: older adult fossils begin to outnumber younger adult fossils. As Maggie Koerth-Baker writes in the *New York Times Magazine*,

> This demographic shift coincided with an explosion of cultural production: clay figurines, carvings made of bone, wood and stone; cave art and jewelry making; and complex burial practices. According to Caspari, it was longer human life spans that seem to have made this flourishing possible. Having more time on earth allows our species to progress.

Thus, we can see some connection between advanced age and human culture. But in subsequent millennia, there would be times of greater or lesser life expectancy. Changes in climate and diet would have impacts in the medieval and early modern periods.

The French anthropologist Maurice Godelier summarizes a global literature that sees some recognition of elders between 40 and 60 or 65. His own fieldwork among the Baruya of Papua New Guinea describes some in their 40s as mature authorities, with old age setting in around 50, although those who had been great warriors or shamans could enjoy authoritative roles considerably longer (Godelier, p. 17). Among hunter-gatherers there was presumably a sexual division of labor whereby men hunted and women gathered; one may speculate about the consequences for those who survived into a period of disability. Men faced the greater challenge but also operated from a favored position. Women played a greater role in societies that privileged matrilineal descent, such as the Nagovisi of Bougainville in Papua New Guinea or the Na in southern China (p. 24). Of course, physical or cognitive decline may weaken authority greatly, and contact with more "developed" cultures may weaken spiritual power and control over education of the young.

Historians and anthropologists have both had something to say about old age in the African past. The authors of the *Cambridge History of Africa* applied what they had learned from anthropology to describe migrations and contacts among different sub-Saharan peoples and the characteristics of their social orders. These included populations in the Rift Valley of East Africa before 1600 whose organization consisted of "age-sets (*rika*), composed of persons circumcised at the same time, and generation sets (*kambi*), composed of groups of age-sets, changing at intervals of approximately forty to forty-five years" (Vol. 3, p. 666). Studies of the Guinea Coast in West Africa in the seventeenth and eighteenth centuries also find age-grades and secret societies (Vol. 4). Back east in Kenya at the same time, age-set organization played an important military role, as it did among the Zulu in southern Africa after 1790. Age-regiments evolved into standing armies, as they incorporated those they conquered into their organizations. Of course, the basis of such organization was a group of young men, and life expectancy wasn't very high, but those who aged together had a common experience and some hope of becoming elders (Vol. 5).

It is likely that the shift to agriculture in the Neolithic, beginning around 7000 BCE, meant extension of and improvement in the lives of the aged. They no longer had to keep up with younger migrants, and ownership of property would have enhanced the status of some elders. Peter Stearns has hypothesized a shift from taking information from elders to taking information from traders, but maintaining a balance between local authority and communication with others must have been a common challenge (Stearns, "Elders in World History," p. 377). Control of property and taking on priestly and leadership roles, as Simmons had described, would have been key. Some women would also have gained some social power in advancing age. Stearns sums up the situation on the long eve before the emergence of the great urban civilizations: "Property control, a surrounding culture that urged devotion toward older parents, plus some specialized functions for older men in politics and religion – these are virtual commonplaces of cultures and civilizations formed on the basis of agriculture in Asia, Europe, and Africa" (p. 378).

We will turn to urban civilizations in the next chapter, but we should keep in mind that even in Europe, the majority of the population would continue to work in agriculture until the nineteenth century, so issues of family work, with different but complementary tasks performed by men and women, would remain central in the experience of the aged. Methodologically, European family history saw coordination between history and anthropology in the study of household, kinship, and community right down to the onset of industrialization. And cultural anthropologists and cultural historians interacted in creative ways. In a sense, historians were parting company with sociology and teaming up with cultural anthropology. They were doing so at a time when anthropologists were voicing concerns about the nature of their own discipline, partly about its production of a particular form of "literary" (as well as scientific) representation, but particularly about its role in European colonialism. Thus, they looked back to classic works of the nineteenth and early twentieth centuries and saw how the cultures of the "primitive" colonized were contrasted with Western civilization and how ethnographic knowledge at least in part contributed to efforts at imperial control.

The self-consciousness that characterized cultural anthropology extended to its investigations into aging. Ethnographers began to recognize that they had always been confronted with age. Their informants tended to be older individuals, so they paid a bit more attention to the anthropology of old age. Subsequently they tried to explore the anthropology of age (not just the aged). The variety of that work was impressive in locating diverse cultural practices, and they shared a sense of pioneering a new field. Yet, medical anthropologist Lawrence Cohen offered a critique of that literature, building upon the general concern about cultural representation and power and seeing younger, Western anthropologists still examining the aged as outsiders. What was missing was the internal or subjective view. That would come even later, as would an anthropological approach that took account of historical contexts.

Scholars have juxtaposed what they know from contemporary anthropology and what they know from prehistory. There's a tendency to read back into the deep past what is observed among tribal groups that survive into the present (a "regressive" method). But we need to be aware of the often subtle interactions between those groups and modernity. Indeed, we will come back to those issues at the end of the book. For it will be useful to think not only in terms of social security crises, Alzheimer's, and the modern, individual life course. We should also recognize the confrontation that occurs between people living in different cultural worlds simultaneously. To take just one example, Michael David McNally describes how a revival of North American Indian ways of aging was prompted by the experience of the contemporary world. Thus, what was "traditional" was not denied but in some ways strengthened.

But before we return to the present, our task in this book is to explore the past. And with early city dwelling we have written records. We will use them for a two-fold purpose. We will want to understand how older people acted and were perceived by others, and we will want to understand how classic texts formed ways of thinking about age that would be taken up by their successors, even down to the present.

Works Cited and Further Reading

Simone de Beauvoir, *La vieillesse* (Paris: Gallimard, 1970), English translation *The Coming of Age* (NY: Putnam, 1972); Leo Simmons, *The Role of the Aged in Primitive Society* (New Haven: Yale University Press, 1945); James G. Flanagan, "Hierarchy in Simple 'Egalitarian' Societies," *Annual Review of Anthropology*, Vol. 18 (1989): 245–266; Paul Spencer, *The Samburu: A Study of Gerontocracy in a Nomadic Tribe* (Berkeley: University of California Press, 1965); Dennis Werner, "Gerontocracy among the Mekranoti of Central Brazil," *Anthropological Quarterly*, Vol. 54, No. 1 (Jan., 1981): 15–27; Kim Hill and A. Magdalena Hurtado, *Ache Life History: The Ecology and Demography of a Foraging People* (NY: Aldine de Gruyter, 1996); Nancy Howell, *Life Histories of the Dobe!Kung: Food, Fatness, and Well-being Over the Life Span* (Berkeley: University of California Press, 2010); Michael Gurven and Hillard Kaplan, "Longevity among Hunter-Gatherers: A Cross-Cultural Examination," *Population and Development Review*, Vol. 33, No. 2 (June 2007): 321–365; Claude Masset, "Prehistory of the Family," in *A History of the Family*, Vol. 1, *Distant Worlds, Ancient Worlds*, edited by André Burguière, Christiane Klapisch-Zuber, Martine Segalen, and Françoise Zonabend (Cambridge: Harvard University Press, 1996).

Rachel Caspari and Sang-Hee Lee, "Older Age Becomes Common Late in Human Evolution," *PNAS*, July 27, 2004, Vol. 10, No. 30 {www.pnas.org/content/101/30/10895.full.pdf}; Caspari, "The Evolution of Grandparents," *Scientific American*, August 2011; Maggie Koerth-Baker, "Who Lives Longest?" *New York Times Magazine*, March 19, 2013.

Maurice Godelier, "De la vieillesse magnifiée à la vieillesse marginalisée et même expulsée du monde des vivants," in Maurice Godelier, François Jullien, and Joseph Maïla, *Le grand âge de la vie* (Paris: PUF, 2005). The pertinent volumes in the *Cambridge History of Africa* (Cambridge: Cambridge University Press) were edited as follows: Vol. 3, edited by Roland Oliver (1977); Vol. 4, edited by Richard Gray (1975); Vol. 5, edited by John E. Flint (1976). Peter N. Stearns, "Elders in World History," chapter 16 in *Handbook of the Humanities and Aging*, edited by Thomas R. Cole, David D. Van Tassel, and Robert Kastenbaum (NY: Springer, 1992).

For the influence of anthropology on the practice of history, see, for example, Hans Medick and David Sabean, eds., *Interest and Emotion: Essays on the Study of*

Family and Kinship (Cambridge: Cambridge University Press, 1984). A very influential work on anthropology and writing is James Clifford and George E. Marcus, eds., *Writing Culture: The Poetics and Politics of Ethnography* (Berkeley: University of California Press, 1986; 25th anniversary edition, 2009). Among the works by anthropologists that explored their profession's complicity in the colonial enterprise are Talal Asad, ed., *Anthropology and the Colonial Encounter* (Atlantic Highlands, NJ: Humanities Press, 1973, 6th printing 1992), and Adam Kuper, *The Reinvention of Primitive Society: Transformations of a Myth* (London: Routledge, 2005), a revision of a book first published in 1988 under the title *The Invention of Primitive Society: Transformations of an Illusion*. Important anthropological approaches to aging and the aged include Pamela T. Amoss and Stevan Harrell, eds., *Other Ways of Growing Old: Anthropological Perspectives* (Stanford: Stanford University Press, 1981); David I. Kertzer and Jennie Keith, eds., *Age and Anthropological Theory* (Ithaca: Cornell University Press, 1984); and Christine L. Fry, ed., *Aging in Culture and Society: Comparative Viewpoints and Strategies* (NY: Praeger, 1980). For an important critique, see Lawrence Cohen, "Old Age: Cultural and Critical Perspectives," *Annual Review of Anthropology*, Vol. 23 (1994): 137–158. For an anthropology that demonstrates awareness of historical contexts, see many of the contributions to *Transitions and Transformations: Cultural Perspectives on Aging and the Life Course*, edited by Caitrin Lynch and Jason Danely (NY and Oxford: Berghahn Books, 2013). Michael David McNally, *Aging, Authority, and Ojibwe Religion* (NY: Columbia University Press, 2009).

3

OLD AGE IN CLASSICAL CIVILIZATIONS: FROM ASIA TO THE NEAR EAST AND MEDITERRANEAN

Classical civilizations in Asia, the Near East, and the Mediterranean all had something to say about old age. They offered models for living, aging, and dying over centuries, even millennia. It is our task to understand their own contexts as well as forms of thought and representation that long outlived them. In many ways, the terms of discussion of old age were set over the long term, and we have an opportunity to consider their common characteristics and how they continue to provide models for modern and contemporary thinking about aging and the aged. For that reason, this chapter and the next will quote more freely from texts of the period studied than will other chapters.

In the Western world, we may think automatically of Greece and Rome, of Hippocrates, Socrates, Cicero, and Seneca. But we also have an almost equally automatic urge to contrast Mediterranean antiquity with the ancient civilizations of Asia, which are often presented as more respectful of old age. That assumption carries over to the present in the form of suspicions that in South Asia and East Asia, "traditional" veneration of the aged survived longer and ran deeper than anything found in Europe or the Americas. Despite important countervailing tendencies, Hinduism and Confucianism continue to form constituent elements of Indian and Chinese culture in their home countries and diasporas. Anthropologists Pamela Amoss and Stevan Harrell offer a stark contrast between them.

> That Indian elders are enjoined to go begging in the forest as part of a search for wisdom, whereas Chinese elders ideally remain at home surrounded by crowds of grandchildren, reflects not environmental conditions but the different religious ideals of the two great Asian civilizations.
>
> *(Amoss and Harrell, p. 23)*

On both counts, that may be an exaggeration. Let us begin with India, whose elders have never all left their homes in search of wisdom. Hinduism has always balanced asceticism and family values. The early Aryan peoples (defined linguistically, not racially) who entered India from the northwest as far back as 1500 BCE carried with them the ancient *Veda* to be recited at sacrificial ceremonies and to guarantee good health and protection. Historians don't see them as founding Indian civilization—archaeological remains suggest earlier Indus-valley origins—but the emerging literary culture included ideas that would have a long-term impact. The *Rig Veda* presented a worldly old age: "Let me be lord over this world, with good cattle and good sons; let me see and win a long life-span and enter old age as if going home" (1.116). As one scholar of comparative religion puts it, the religion of the Aryans in India "placed a strong emphasis on life enhancement and life extension" (Thursby, p. 182).

An enthusiastic expression of this confidence in sacrificial ritual as a means of securing a ripe old age is found in *Atharna Veda* 19.67:

> For a hundred autumns may we see,
> For a hundred autumns may we live,
> For a hundred autumns may we know,
> For a hundred autumns may we rise,
> For a hundred autumns may we flourish
> For a hundred autumns may we be,
> For a hundred autumns may we become,
> —and even more than a hundred autumns!
> *(R. Panikkar, ed. and trans.,* The Vedic Experience *[Berkeley: University of California Press, 1977], as quoted in Thursby, pp. 182–183)*

A change is observed around 600 BCE away from the idea of long life as essentially good. The later Vedic view involved endless recurrence. Life becomes an ascetic, disciplined, and meditative experience, a cycle of pain and suffering, as expressed in the *Upanishads*. Here is the ideal identified by Amoss and Harrell, but it's not necessarily limited to the elderly: "Sparsely inhabited forests and hills, therefore, became places for retreat from the world, where people of all ages sought spiritual realization to effect a route of escape from the otherwise endless cycles of rebirth" (Thursby, p. 184). As a prayer in the *Chandogya Upanishad* put it: "May I, who am the glory of the glories, not go to hoary and toothless, yea to toothless and driveling [old age]! Yea, may I not go to driveling [old age]!" Thus, there was an effort to escape the ravages of age and of the world. As the Hindu tradition continued to evolve, it balanced worldliness and asceticism. By 200 BCE, the *Bhagavad Gita* was reinterpreting Vedic sacrifice and Upanishadic renunciation.

Recent social scientists working on contemporary Indian aging claim to see anticipations of modern issues of social welfare in the distant past, but scholars of ancient and medieval India have questioned the Western idealization of Asian aging. Joachim F. Sprockhoff and Albrecht Wezler have raised the possibility that the so-called ideal of retreat was rooted in an earlier practice of abandonment. There are suggestions of younger generations taking authority from aged parents, offering minimal support, and pushing elders out. Moreover, the philosophical and literary texts that provide almost the only evidence for much of this history referred essentially to elites (Wezler, pp. 37–63).

The emergent Indian social system divided the population into castes. At the top were the three "twice-born" castes (*Brahman, Kshatriya, Vaishya*), who were eligible to learn the Veda and to experience the four stages (*ashrama*) of the life course. The first two were student and householder. The third, *Vanaprastha ashrama*, was the senior couple that, upon the birth of grandsons, made a transition to "a more retiring and contemplative mode of life together" (Thursby, p. 186). A few entered the ideal fourth stage, *Sannyasa ashrama*, when elders turned solitary wanderers and engaged in retreat from the world and from family.

Brahmanic focus on the spirit and disdain for the body should not keep us from recognizing the importance of competing ideas and of an ancient Indian medical tradition. The early Vedic period (ca. 1700–800 BCE), according to Kenneth Zysk, discussed healing in a magico-religious context. For him, the emergence of an Indian medical science of *ayurveda*, with its key classical treatises produced ca. 200 BCE to 400 CE, depended upon a Buddhist influence and the work of heterodox ascetics. Buddhist monasteries were places for the development of more empirical and rational medical thought. It can be distinguished from the brahmanic disdain for the body. "The connection between heterodox, particularly Buddhist, asceticism and medicine is perhaps best illustrated through anatomy. The approach of the early Buddhists and the physicians to an understanding of the human body reflects both a commitment to materialism through empiricism and rationality and a firm rejection of brahmanic orthodoxy" (Zysk, p. 34). *Ayurveda* itself means "the science of longevity," and it has continued to be an important medical tradition even as Muslim migration brought *unani* (Ionian or Greek) medicine to India in the twelfth century, European travelers brought their medicine in the early modern period, and the British bore "modern" cosmopolitan medicine in the nineteenth century. But it was a Chinese traveler in the early fifth century CE, Fa-hsien, who reported on an Indian hospital, and we know of a great many hospitals in South Asia before the arrival of European physicians (Basham, p. 34). One of the earliest *ayurvedic* texts, that of Caraka, rejected notions of a predetermined lifespan, explaining that

> the lifespan that creatures have depends upon a combination of factors. Its strength or weakness is based on fate, as well as human agency, fate being the karma one created oneself during a previous embodiment, and

human agency being thought of as what further karma one creates at the present time.

(Carakasamhita, cited in Wujastyk, p. 39)

That treatise divided medicine into eight branches: general medicine, treatment of body parts above the shoulders, surgery, toxicology, possession, pediatrics, life-preserving tonics, and aphrodisiacs. In general the *ayurvedic* texts spoke of humors (*dosas*), constituent parts (*dhatus*), and excretions and secretions (*malas*) (Benner, pp. 3852–3858). Vedic imagery and mythology may still appear in the early medical classics, but the new emphasis is on the material body.

For all of its openness to knowledge about the body, Buddhism, both in India and China, also involved renunciation of the world. Gautama the Buddha (ca. 560–480 BCE) emphasized monasticism and used old age as a source of moral lessons. Indeed, old age was painful to behold:

> When old age shatters the body, gradually the limbs become loose; the old person's teeth decay and fall out; he becomes covered with wrinkles and sinews and veins; he can't see far, and the pupils of his eyes are fixed in space; tufts of hair appear in his nostrils, and his body trembles. All his bones become prominent; his back and joints are bent; and since his digestive fire has gone out, he eats little and moves little. It is only with pain and difficulty that he walks, rises, lies down, sits, and moves, and his hearing and sight become sluggish; his mouth is smeared with oozing saliva. As he looks toward death, all of his senses are no longer controlled; and he cannot remember even important things that he had experienced at that very moment.
>
> *(W.D. O'Flaherty, ed. and trans., Textual Sources for the Study of Hinduism [Totowa, NJ: Barnes and Noble, 1988], pp. 100–101, as excerpted by Thursby, p. 189)*

Among the sights that Gautama saw that turned him from the world were those of a decrepit old man, a sick man, and a dead man. Turning away from the world meant turning away from self. For his followers, this meant a lack of anxiety surrounding aging and death, just a focus on mindfulness. In our own day Buddhist practices obviously survive and have crossed over to Western aging, especially in palliative care. In present-day Thailand, Buddhist culture encourages children's obligations to repay their aged parents. "*Katanyu Katawethi*" refers to parent–child relationships; "*Bunkun*" refers to broader social connections. At least in recent times daughters are often more responsible than sons for care of aged parents (Pussayapibul, Srithamrongsawat, and Bundhamcharoen, p. 167).

By contrast, Confucianism in China emphasized filial piety (that of the son), the performance of ritual, and veneration of ancestors. The ideal was social harmony in a world characterized by strong familial structures. Historical memory was a part of this ideal, as Confucius saw the Zhou Dynasty (1050–700 BCE) as a golden age of harmony. Harmony between generations was important as well for Mencius (372–289 BCE), but Xunzi (298?–238 BCE) encouraged filial piety and ancestor worship. François Jullien points out that the ancient Chinese thought about aging in a way that was fundamentally different from the approach of Western philosophers: a process of change and transition that involved simultaneous modification (*bian*) and continuation (*tong*), not the Western shift from one state to another. A Taoist approach by Zhuangzi speaks of the fatigue of life, the release that comes with old age, and the repose that comes with death. Old age is viewed as welcoming rather than unhappy or repugnant. Being held by life and released by old age corresponds to the respiration of the world. Confucian thought presented old age as a culmination, longevity of vital potential being the key rather than immortality.

In the words attributed to Confucius:

> At fifteen I set my heart upon learning.
> At thirty I established myself [in accordance with ritual].
> At forty I no longer had perplexities.
> At fifty I knew the Mandate of Heaven.
> At sixty I was at ease with whatever I heard.
> At seventy I could follow my heart's desire without transgressing the boundaries of right.
> *(Confucius,* Analects, *as excerpted in* The Oxford Book of Aging, *pp. 26–27)*

A first-century CE autobiography of a provincial sub-prefect describes his definitive break with the world of public service. Wang Chong (27 CE to ca. 100 CE) had already begun to withdraw as he had grown older. At around seventy,

> he gave up his official carriage, and his official career was definitely closed. He could not help it. He had many annoyances, and his body felt the infirmities of age. His hair grew white, his teeth fell out, he became older from day to day, and his comrades dispersed. He had nothing to rely upon, was too poor to nurse himself, and had no joy left. But time went slowly on, the *geng* and *xing* years came to an end, but though he was afraid that his death was near at hand, he was still full of silly ideas. Then he wrote a book on Macrobiotics in sixteen chapters.
>
> To keep himself alive, he cherished the vital fluid. As a stimulant for the appetite he used wine. Closing eyes and ears against external influences, he spared his energy as a means of self-protection. Using medicines he kept up his forces, and by following this method he hoped to prolong his days. For a while he did not age, but when it was too late, there was no return.
> *(Wang Ch'ung, p. 82)*

As in other ancient civilizations, we often know more about male officials than about women or laborers.

More than the individual life course, as we have seen, Confucian China devoted much attention to filial piety (*Xiao*), the logograph for which consists of a man above a boy. Traditionally, it is read as a symbol of the central ethical value of caring for and revering parents in life and death, continuing to honor their wishes after their passing and having progeny to continue support of ancestors in future generations. According to Confucius: "In serving his parents, a filial son reveres them in daily life; he makes them happy while he nourishes them; he takes anxious care of them in sickness; he shows great sorrow over their death; and he sacrifices to them with solemnity" (Ikels, ed., *Filial Piety*, p. 3). Chinese thought presented filial piety as the fundamental value, the basis of all social, cultural, and even political connections, including one's relationship to state authority. The Confucian-era *Book of Filial Piety* explained that "filial piety commences with service to parents; it proceeds with service to the sovereign; it is completed by the establishment of one's own personality" (*Oxford Book of Aging*, p. 106).

Confucius' ideal of "nourishing the old" appears time and time again in classical texts. For example, Mencius refers to those who follow King Wen because they have heard that "the chief of the West knows well how to nourish the old" (Mencius, p. 180). And he describes a sovereign's tour of inspection of his princes as follows:

> When the sovereign entered the boundaries of a State, if the new ground was being reclaimed, and the old fields well cultivated; if the old were nourished and the worthy honoured; and if men of distinguished talents were placed in office: then the prince was rewarded – rewarded with an addition to his territory.
>
> *(p. 312)*

Neglect of the old was evidence of unworthiness. The *Wang Zhi* (Royal Regulations) chapter of the *Li ji* (Record of Rites), one of the Five Classics of the Confucian canon elaborates on the ideal:

> The kings of the three dynasties, in nourishing the old, always had the years of those connected with them brought to their notice. Where (an officer) was eighty, one of his sons was free from all duties of government service; where he was ninety, all the members of his family were set free from them.
>
> *(Legge, Li Ki, Book III, p. 243)*

Nourishment was both symbolic and literal, and it extended to the deceased, as in a college ceremony described in the *Wen Wang Shi Zi* (King Wen as Son and Heir) chapter of the *Li ji*:

> When the son of Heaven was about to visit the college, the drum was beaten at early dawn to arouse all (the students). When all were come together, the son of Heaven then arrived and ordered the proper officers to discharge their business, proceeding in the regular order, and sacrificing to the former masters and former Sages. When they reported to him that everything had been done, he then began to go to the nourishing (of the aged). Proceeding to the school on the east, he unfolded and set forth the offerings to the aged of former times, and immediately afterwards arranged the mats and places for the three (classes of the) old, and the five (classes of the) experienced, for all the aged (indeed who were present). He (then) went to look at the food and examine the liquor. When the delicacies for the nourishment of the aged were all ready, he caused the song to be raised (as a signal for the aged to come). After this he retired and thus it was that he provided for (the aged) his filial nourishment.
>
> (Legge, Li Ki, Book VI, pp. 359–360)

In connection with such ceremonial expressions of respect for the aged, the *Nei Ze* (The Patterns of the Family) chapter of the *Li ji* describes increasing honor with each decade:

> For those of fifty, the grain was (fine and) different (from that used by younger men). For those of sixty, there was meat kept in store (from the day before). For those of seventy, there was a second service of savoury meat. Those of eighty were supplied regularly with delicacies. For those of ninety, food and drink were never out of their chambers; wherever they wandered, it was deemed right that savoury meat and drink should follow them.
>
> (Legge, Li Ki, Book X, p. 465)

Such differences in treatment were a recognition of bodily decline:

> At fifty, one was supposed to begin to decay; at sixty, not to feel satisfied unless he had flesh to eat. At seventy, he was thought to require silk in order to make him feel warm; at eighty, to need some one (to sleep) with him, to keep him warm; and at ninety, not to feel warm even with that.
>
> (Ibid.)

Public ceremonies were thought to model proper behavior in private life. As the *Xiang Yin Jiu Yi* (The Meaning of the Drinking Festivity in the Districts) chapter of the *Li ji* puts it:

> At the ceremony of drinking in the country districts, those who were sixty years old sat, and those who were (only fifty) stood, and were in waiting to receive any orders and perform any services – thus illustrating the honour

which should be paid to elders. Before those who were sixty, three dishes were placed; before those of seventy, four; before those of eighty, five; before those of ninety, six – thus illustrating how the aged should be cherished and nourished. When the people knew to honour their elders and nourish their aged, then at home they could practise filial piety and fraternal duty. Filial and fraternal at home and abroad, honouring elders and nourishing the aged, then their education was complete, and this led to the peace and tranquility of the state.

(Legge, Li Ki, Book XLII, pp. 439–440)

A third-century CE text indicates that adherence to the ideal of filial piety might even be used in resisting demands of a forgetful state. Li Mi describes a history of illness and tragedy that led to his having been brought up by his grandmother, who now needs his attention. He must decline an offer of state offices and honors:

My grandmother is now in the sunset of her days, and, with faint breath, she seems likely to come to the end of her life at every moment. Without my grandmother, I would not have been able to live today, and without me, my grandmother would have no one to comfort her old age. In fact, we, grandmother and grandson, have been depending upon each other for life. This is my humble reason why I cannot leave her behind.

(Oxford Book of Aging, pp. 114–116)

Reciprocity is a key element in the relationship.

Studies of modern Chinese aging all begin with the traditional ideal of filial piety and ask to what extent Chinese cultures have kept it alive. We will address the question later, and we will also explore how ancient Chinese medical thought, a humoral system comparable to Galenic medicine in the West and Ayurvedic medicine in South Asia, survives in the modern world. It spread from China to Korea, Japan, and Vietnam before making its way around the world, often travelling with Chinese philosophy.

In her history of old age, Simone de Beauvoir considers China the great exception in the ancient world, the place where veneration of the aged held strong for centuries. She tied it to a relatively unchanging society with a well-developed state and a hydraulic economy. Although Chinese literati were inclined to claim strict continuity with the past and filial piety remained a rhetorically important value in all ages, its expression in actual practice could vary as economic and social conditions changed from region to region or from era to era. Confucianism was reemphasized in the T'ang Dynasty (618–906), with its support for parental authority. And the T'ang code survived in a thirteenth-century version that declared that "those who lifted a hand against parents or grandparents deserved to be beheaded" (Beauvoir, p. 98). Michel Cartier refers to the Chinese family as an intermediary between society and government. He describes the Ming (1368–1644) and Qing

(1645–1911) as involving a stable balance between family and state and a legal code that paid attention to relative ages. "Under the Ming dynasty, especially in the beginning, special dignity was conferred on men aged over sixty as 'elders' on whom official insignia had been bestowed" (Cartier, p. 516). We'll return to the East in the next chapter, with looks at Japan and the Islamic world. But for now we move west to Mesopotamia, Egypt, Greece, and Rome.

Some evidence for Mesopotamia comes from non-literary sources. They include Akkadian administrative literature and a vendor list on an obelisk. "The 'elders' certainly enjoyed authority over the whole of the social body: the Akkadian term of *shibum* meant both 'elder' and 'notable'" (Glassner, p. 100).

Rivkah Harris, who has done the most to elucidate the theme of aging in Mesopotamia, cites a text from the seventh century BCE that resembles other classical and early modern treatments of the ages of life:

> Forty (years mean) prime of life
> Fifty: short life
> Sixty: maturity
> Seventy: long life
> Eighty: old age
> Ninety: extreme old age.
>
> *(Harris, p. 28)*

As in those other treatments, this text doesn't represent a typical experience. It does, however, posit a maximum expectation and a recognition that old age took various forms.

Other Mesopotamian texts refer to the desire for long life (p. 30) and an ideal life span of 120. For Harris, to live longer in health and happiness was a Mesopotamian desire, with none of the resentments that would emerge in Greek culture, but while the language used to describe aging and the aged referred to lasting and traveling, it also mentioned helplessness and powerlessness (p. 52). Thus, one can already see the duality of young–old and old–old. Scholars suggest that elite men and women lived longer than non-elites, and Harris singles out "cloistered women dedicated to the god Shamash of Sippar in the Old Babylonian period" (p. 53) as frequently living past their 60s. Ancient texts speak of long life accompanied by good health as a reward for virtue. A memorial stele offers the voice of an exceptional (if not unbelievable) old woman of 104 with keen senses and good digestion and spirits (p. 55). She had supposedly lived to see great-great-grandchildren. Other texts offered much less happy experiences. They spoke of loss of vigor and sexual potency, loss of teeth, inability to control urine flow, etc. They suggested that alcohol could combat depression in old age, and while they depicted respect for the wisdom of the aged, they engaged in ridicule of overly talkative elders.

Literary texts contrasted "the cautiousness and restraint of the old against the impulsiveness and risk taking of the young" (p. 70). As the elders say in the *Epic of Gilgamesh*: "You are young, Gilgamesh, [and] your enthusiasm carries you away." Yet Mesopotamian myths "counter[ed] the idealization of the elderly and old age, focusing instead on the injustices perpetrated by the old against the young" (p. 73). Harris reads the *Enuma Elish*, the Mesopotamian creation myth, "as a justification for granting the young (namely Marduk) the possibility of assuming power. ... This myth emphasizes paternal (and maternal) hostility toward offspring, challenging the authority and wisdom of the old" (p. 74). Yet, Marduk's reign is seen as resolving conflict and creating mutuality: "the old must cede or at least share their privileges with the young; in return the young are to provide for and protect the old." Of course we are in the realm of myth. Expressions of mutuality may represent peaceful relations but may also seem to mitigate very real intergenerational tensions. Indeed, the myth emphasizes the triumph of young Marduk over the old goddess Tiamat.

But Tiamat is hardly everywoman, and Mesopotamian writings, like those in other civilizations to come, identified a shift in women's lives at menopause. The Akkadian and Sumerian languages had terms to describe those whose blood had stopped flowing, and Harris concludes that "the cessation of menstruation probably brought about a positive change in later life" (p. 92). Some older women performed ritual tasks, as they were no longer considered impure, and they also served as intercessors, advisors, brewers of beer, dream interpreters, healers, and mourners. Gilgamesh is advised by the old woman Siduri and his own mother, Ninsun; several queen mothers are also well known to have advised their sons. Because of the difference in age between husbands and wives, widowhood was common and, especially for non-elites, a serious challenge; a high rate of remarriage has been hypothesized. Whether or not they remarried, they presumably played a role as grandmothers, but literary texts referred more often to grandfathers, as with the god Anu offering his grandson Marduk the four winds.

Enough evidence survives from ancient Egypt to provide a somewhat nuanced view of old age. The Instructions of Ptahotep include a lament over the weakness and infirmities of advanced age; however, several inscriptions suggest an Egyptian ideal of living 110 years (Forgeau, p. 148). Blue-green amulets were worn both to delay old age and, after death, to achieve eternal youth. Hieroglyphics represented "old" and "growing old" through images of curved silhouettes. We have no evidence of people actually living out the ideal 110 years, but commemorative inscriptions do mention lives as long as 90. Some writings evoke intergenerational responsibilities: the scribe Ani writes that "children should acknowledge the debt they owe their mother: 'Nourish your mother as she nourished you, sustain her in the same way as she bore you'" (p. 151). Widows could manage household and property, exercising the authority of husbands and temporarily taking over authority of eldest sons. Annie Forgeau cites an artisan's wife from Deir el-Medineh

> who disinherited three of her children from her second marriage because they had neglected her in her old age: 'I will not give any of my property to

those who have given me nothing'….The common practice of providing accommodation for a widowed parent is reflected in texts stressing the proper manner for children to behave.

(p. 152)

Connections can be drawn between Mesopotamian and Egyptian cultures and the ancient Hebrew culture that would have a long-term influence on centuries of Jewish, Christian, and Muslim life. The Hebrew Bible refers to some of the earliest figures living hundreds of years (Methuselah, for example), but even as more credible ages came to be reported, the overarching themes remained those of authority and respect. Readers were to honor parents: "Honor your father and your mother, that you may live long in the land which the Lord your God is giving you," *Exodus*: 20.12. More generally they were to honor gray hairs. "Rise before the aged and show deference to the old," *Leviticus*: 19.32. "Gray hair is a crown of glory, and it is won by a virtuous life," *Proverbs*: 16.31. *Proverbs* (23.22) and *Psalms* (71.9) warned against abandonment of the aged. Even though it was possible to portray a patriarch, such as Isaac, as a feeble and blind old man, the emphasis was on long life as a reward for fulfilling the covenant. Harold M. Stahmer, deploying Biblical language himself, presents Hebrew old age as a reward "for having walked in the ways of the Lord all their lives" (Stahmer, p. 31).

Patriarchy (along with the representation of accompanying matriarchs) loomed large for centuries, and elders were said to wield religious and judicial power. That power seemed to continue into the era of early kings and then saw some decline. Yet, according to Sheldon Isenberg, there was a role for elders through the period of the First Temple, as they continued to appoint kings and declare war (Isenberg, p. 152).

Prophetic writings preserved the theme of adoration of the old and serve as reminders of how things presumably used to be. But later texts also admit the difficulties of aging. Minois quotes *Lamentations* and *Ezekiel* to connect the period of exile with a turning against the aged and of elders no longer exercising traditional roles. The destruction of the First Temple (traditionally 586 BCE), the loss of political autonomy, and the pain of exile meant separation from the site of the ancient cult and increasing dependence upon text. Some scholars argue that the emergence of writing meant weakening of the position of the aged as repositories of tradition and wisdom. That probably held true for the Hebrews, but those written texts themselves preserved the idea of respect for the aged.

Some of the movement away from idealizing advanced age may be the result of Hellenistic influence. *Kohelet/Ecclesiastes* offers a metaphorical description of bodily decline: "the keepers of the house (the arms) shall tremble, the strong men (the legs) shall bow themselves, the grinders (the teeth) cease because they are few, those that look out of the window (the eyes) are darkened, the shutters (the ears) are closed" (*Ecclesiastes* 12.3). Physical weakness is accompanied by fear, spiritual decline, and eventual death. Real problems and fears are recounted. *Tobit*

8.7 refers to an old couple's fears of seeing each other die, and *Siracid/Ecclesiasticus* 3.12–13 calls for patience to be shown the aged father. Thus, for those following in the tradition, honor of the aged continues, but for those looking for historical evidence, warnings against dishonor suggest disrespect.

It is common to see the Christian emphasis on youth combating elders as a way of separating Christianity from Judaism, but it may also have grown out of Hebraic elements that were no longer so positive about old age. Those elements were the result of both historical experience and Greek influence, which Georges Minois describes as a process that desacralized and trivialized the old man.

> Hebrew thought no longer envisaged him as more than an aged, suffering and diminished man, waiting for death. His longevity, previously the source of his prestige, now only served to increase his culpability when he committed faults. The type of odious, garrulous, senile, disgusting and lascivious old man which occurs so frequently in Greek comedies, was in process of penetrating Jewish life.
>
> *(Minois, p. 38)*

Minois sees the old man as "only an image, a symbol" (p. 39), identified more and more with God rather than human experience. Thus, Jewish history becomes characterized by an ambiguity between traditional images and texts and a less idealized reality.

The idea that a decline in Judaism's view of the aged resulted from Hellenistic influence suggests something about Greek aging. Minois titles his chapter on the Greeks "Sad Old Age." Greek mythology reported incredibly long lives in the distant past, Greek memory included that of Homer's aged Nestor, King of Pylos, as a symbol of wisdom, and Greek imagery offered some positive representations of aged philosophers, but the positive representation tends to be overwhelmed by images of old age as loathsome and youth, particularly male youth, as beautiful. Sparta may have been a gerontocracy, with its council of elders (*gerousia*), but the council's power was not unlimited, and eventually younger officials took control. No other city-state came close to absolute rule by elders, and Athens was very far from it.

Nevertheless, *gerousiai* existed in a range of city-states (*poleis*), and recent study of the Greek east finds them as late as the Hellenistic and Roman periods. Historians debate whether they were primarily political or social organizations; Ennio Bauer, having looked at four regions (Caria, Lycia, Pamphylia, and Pisidia), sees them as expressing "an age consciousness of the older members of the society of the Hellenistic and Roman *poleis*." For him they are "associations which actively participated in the social, religious, and political life of their *poleis*" (Bauer, p. 130). Thus, they were both political and social. He estimates that members were in their 50s and older (p. 135) and that they had at least some social standing even if they were not all drawn from the elite. Thus, old age was important but not determinant in matters of authority. Such bodies had a role in honoring notable individuals and benefactors (pp. 144–145), mediated between council and assembly (p. 149), and offered a space for some old men to engage in civic life (p. 151).

Some Greek thinkers linked age to wisdom. Plato's *Republic* saw advancing age as freeing people from physical desire, and his character of Cephalus offered an occasion to link aging, virtue, and happiness. Cephalus tells Socrates that character trumps age. "For if men are sensible and good-tempered, old age is easy enough to bear: if not, youth as well as age is a burden" (Minois, p. 58). Moreover, Plato's ideal republic is governed by elders. Still, he recognized the challenges of physical and mental weakness.

Observation of such challenges led Aristotle in a very different direction. His *Rhetoric* paints an unpleasant picture. Tim Parkin summarizes Aristotle as follows:

> Older people are…overly pessimistic, distrustful, malicious, suspicious and small-minded because they have been humbled by life and so their greatest hopes are raised to nothing more than staying alive. They lack generosity, are cowardly and always anticipating danger ('old age paves the way for cowardice'), and yet they also love life to excess, especially on their last day of life.
> (Parkin, "The Ancient Greek and Roman Worlds," p. 57)

Such an image had a very long life.

Some scholars present Plato as offering the ideal and Aristotle the real. But it might be an overstatement to suggest such a neat contrast. In any case, what ancient Greece did provide, within certain socio-economic or political limits, was the richness of human experience. Greek sources extend well beyond philosophy to drama. The chorus of old men in *Oedipus at Colonus* presented a tragic image of advanced age:

> None but a fool would scorn life that was brief.
> None but a fool would cleave to life too long:
> For when an old man draws his lingering breath
> Beyond his fitting season, pain and grief,
> The harsh years' harvesting, upon him throng
> And joy is but a phantom of the past.
> Then soon or late the doom of Hades, death,
> Comes with no dance, no lyre, no marriage song,
> All all alike delivers at the last.
>
> Incomparably best is not to be.
> And next to this, once a man sees the day,
> I wish all speed to hasten whence he came;
> After youth's trifling joy, he is not free,

> He must endure his lot as best he may;
> Envy, sedition, murder, hate and strife,
> Until at length old age, unfriended, lame,
> Reviled and lonely claims him for its pay:
> The wretched ending of a wretched life.
> (Oedipus at Colonus, II. 1166–83, as quoted in
> Minois, pp. 49–50)

Greek comedy heaped scorn at age-inappropriate behavior by the elderly, something the Romans and their imitators would continue.

Greek divisions of the ages of life and medical theories of aging had a long influence. They informed ideas about authority and physical decline. Old age for women was often linked to menopause. The threshold of old age for men was often set at 60, though there was no necessary change in role or authority associated with it. Hippocratic texts, which had a centuries-long influence, described a long process by which the body grew cold and dry. "Knowing" the process meant attempting to stop it, and dietary, environmental, and behavioral recommendations emerged.

The classic book in English devoted to old age in ancient Greece, Bessie Richardson's *Old Age among the Ancient Greeks*, lists examples and offers illustrations, but more recent scholarship claims it extrapolated too much from funerary inscriptions and offered much too optimistic a vision of Greek aging (Catrysse). Some more recent scholarship combines the Greeks and Romans and sees variety in both contexts. Assigned the task of writing on both, Parkin writes, "old age as a personified concept to the Greeks and Romans merited not worship but awe, if not dread" (Parkin, p. 65). He goes on:

> Even for the wealthy elite, with whom most of our surviving evidence is concerned, old age in antiquity tended to be a time to be endured rather than enjoyed. For the poorer classes old age must have been singularly unenviable: it was a common proverb that old age and poverty are both burdensome – in combination they are impossible to bear.
>
> (p. 69)

Thanks to Parkin and others, we now have a fairly rich historical literature that focuses on the aged in Rome. And with the spread of Roman power and civilization, we see influences all around the Mediterranean and reaching deep into the Middle Ages and early modern period. Thomas Falkner and Judith de Luce point out that Roman written records are more copious than Greek, that Roman law provides an important window onto multiple aspects of aging, and that sculptural representation became more realistic in Roman times (Falkner and de Luce, p. 18). They write that the Romans presented "old age as a time of lost opportunities, of physical and mental deterioration" (p. 34) but also as a time of authority if the aged had retained their independence. Parkin writes of "marginalization" of the aged, but others contest that view. Karen Cokayne writes, "Only the old who were weak and decrepit – and who were therefore no longer socially useful – had a marginal status in society" (Cokayne, p. 7).

> An old person could have status, authority and reverence, as long as societal expectations about how life should be lived were fulfilled. Respect for old age had to be earned. Whether or not an old man was able to fulfill his role in society depended largely on his social status, his own personal qualities and his physical and mental fitness.
>
> (p. 179)

According to Cokayne, "the experience of old age was valued in Roman society, and admiration was also shown to those who were no longer physically fit but whose status was assured by their previous deeds and actions" (p. 179).

The Roman demographic world would not have seemed terribly foreign to Westerners as late as the nineteenth century. Ancient historians tell us that life expectancy at birth was around 25 and that if one survived childhood one had a good chance to reach 60. It is estimated that in the first century CE 6–8% of the population of the Roman Empire was over 60, and 2% was over 70 (Parkin, *Old Age in the Roman World*, p. 281), but epidemics changed such static figures. Some age-related norms existed. At 46, the man becomes a *senior*; at around 60, a *senex*. For Ptolemy of Alexandria in the second century CE, the elderly (*presbuteros*) ranged from 56 to 68 and became old (*gerontes*) subsequently (Harlow and Laurence, p. 4). Parkin finds that 65% of senators during the Empire were under the age of 50. But of course there were always some over 60. The ideal emperor was in his 40s or 50s. Exemption from particular posts or services varied from 55 to 65 to 70, but actual decisions about turning away from active life had to do with one's own sense of capacity, "successive withdrawal from work, toil, and military service rather than a simple chronological age of withdrawal." The absolute decline of the body was expected to follow (Harlow and Laurence, p. 4).

Demographic reconstructions suggest that three generations rarely coexisted. Life expectancy at birth was around 25. Men married around 30, women around 20. By age ten, one had a 50% chance of having any grandparents alive, and for obvious reasons maternal grandparents were more common than paternal ones. Difference in age at first marriage had an effect on relationships between husbands and wives. It's not surprising that when many husbands were reaching an age of withdrawal from public life, their wives were reaching the age of menopause. It has been suggested that chronological difference also permitted wives to care for older husbands (Harlow and Laurence, p. 6). There was no law requiring adult children to care for aged parents (as there had been in fifth- and fourth-century BCE

Athens), but it was thought morally proper for generations to see to each other's well-being when necessary. Still, one's lot in old age was generally considered one's own responsibility.

In Rome, the senate would seem to be by definition a council of elders, and there were plenty of old men in public life (Cokayne, p. 95), but some believed in retirement to study or partial retirement. An elite ideal that would be revived later in European history was an intellectually active retirement with dignity (*otium cum dignitate*). In fact senators were generally in charge in their 40s and 50s. Still, there were significant religious roles for the aged. And epitaphs suggest that awareness of advanced age was of some importance. Harlow and Laurence study epitaphs in modern Dougga, ancient Thugga, in modern Tunisia. 48% of commemorated males are over 61. Of females, 42%. (Harlow and Laurence, p. 19): "Hence we should view the evidence of the tombstones of Dougga as demonstrating a value to the old and their longevity." Aging involved a lengthy period of transition, not an automatic change of status or *rite de passage* into old age (Harlow and Laurence, p. 23). To turn again to Parkin,

> The key was not how old, but how active or useful. Cicero's words are timeless, and speak across the millennia: 'Old age will only be respected if it fights for itself, maintains its rights, avoids dependence on anyone, and asserts control over its own to the last breath.'
> *(Parkin, "The Ancient Greek and Roman Worlds," p. 69)*

Unlike some who see positive ideals in the early Republic and negative satirical literature in a later period, Parkin sees different representations coexisting simultaneously, echoing the range of earlier Greek thought. As we have seen, Plato's *Republic* sees advancing age as freeing people from physical desire, and any number of Greeks and Romans could follow his wisdom. Certainly, Cicero in Rome borrowed such ideas. In *De Senectute* (On Old Age), he responded to four common complaints: that the elder is cut off from active life, that the body grows weak, that old age knows no pleasure, and that it is near to death. Cicero emphasized philosophical and age-appropriate activities, and encouraged stoicism in the face of death. The emphasis appears to be on honor, respect, and the maintenance of human dignity. But perhaps this is overly idealized. For Parkin,

> realities are better expressed by Seneca the Younger and Pliny the Elder. Seneca poses a fundamental question:
> "Is the final stage of life the dregs, or is it the clearest and purest part of all, provided only that the mind is unimpaired, and the senses, still sound, give their support to the spirit, and the body is not worn out and dead before its

time? For it makes a great deal of difference whether a man is drawing out his life or his death."

(Parkin, Old Age in the Roman World, pp. 70–71).

He contemplates suicide:

I shall not abandon old age, if old age preserves me intact for myself, and intact as regards the better part of myself; but if old age begins to shatter my mind, and to pull its various faculties to pieces, if it leaves me, not life, but only the breath of life, I shall leap from a building that is crumbling and tottering.

(p. 71)

Continued health was the key to extending careers or enjoying a period of leisure. Pliny distinguishes between late lives of (largely aristocratic) health and tranquility and those that are painful to behold:

Deformed and crippled in every limb, he [Cn. Domitius Tullus] could only enjoy his enormous wealth by contemplating it and could not even turn in bed unless he was man-handled. He also had to have his teeth cleaned and brushed for him – a squalid and pitiful detail. When complaining about the humiliations of his infirmity, he was often heard to say that every day he licked the fingers of his slaves.

(pp. 74–75)

A tradition going back to Aristotle saw the old person as pessimistic, suspicious, and malicious. The satirist Juvenal focuses on "wrinkles, tremulousness, baldness, a runny nose, and loss of teeth" (p. 81). Harlow and Laurence remark that Juvenal's view is that such changes make old people lose their individuality. For scholars of ancient Rome, that seeming uniformity generally involves the drunken old man, the oversexed old woman, infirmity, and disability. Cokayne points out that the still lustful old woman was associated with "foul smells (of breath and of genitals), staining and wetness" (p. 140). The poet Horace penned some of the worst examples. Cokayne writes, "The degrading of the ugly and lascivious old courtesan in obscene language and imagery must be seen as a particular genre of Roman male humour" (p. 142). For Parkin, literary representations were stereotypes that emphasized infirmity. How the stereotypes were related to realities is not such a simple matter, but as Cokayne remarks, "In order to be successful, a stereotype had to strike a chord" (p. 5). Many of them presumably did.

Images mattered. Veristic old age portrait busts showed wrinkles, sunken cheeks, and baldness, representing the "*dignitas* and *gravitas* of age" (Cokayne, p. 18). Masks of elderly ancestors (*imagines*) existed to inspire and teach traditional values. There was some fluctuation: a more classical, idealized image under Augustus, greater naturalism under the Flavians (p. 23). Speech also reflected age. For

Quintilian, an ornate (Asiatic) style was appropriate for youth, a simple (Attic) one for age (p. 30), and the aged were expected to control their emotions (p. 179).

Physiology and appearance are key to Cokayne's study of Roman aging. Romans reported physiological infirmities: "failing eyesight, deafness, catarrhal and respiratory diseases, arthritis, and mental deterioration such as decline in memory and senility." She shows "how the biological decline of the body in ageing, which is basic to every human being, triggered emotional and intellectual changes that had personal, social, political and cultural consequences" (p. 7). The importance for Romans and those who inherited elements of their culture was that such changes described both subjective and objective understandings, the sense of one's own growing old and the external signs that presented others with an image that could inspire respect or revulsion.

Particular old people could represent societal virtues. Even though they might have been exempt from military service, aged men might still behave heroically as in the massacre of old Romans by the Gauls (Aleksandr Koptev, "The Massacre of Old Men," pp. 153–182). And aged women could be exemplars of valued qualities. Thus, Hersilia led the Sabine women in creating Concordia, Veturia, mother of Coriolanus, could force her son to choose between Rome and the Volcians, and aged vestal virgins could gain respect after a 30-year career (Mustakallio, pp. 41–56). A more ordinary Roman woman could aspire to be a respected *matrona* (Cokayne).

When the Romans picked up the Hippocratic tradition on cooling, drying, and degeneration, they modified it in holding out the possibility that old age is not a disease. By the second century CE, "the physician Galen ... saw senescence not as a disease but as a 'midway stage between health and illness', or 'health with a disposition'; he saw disease as contrary to nature, while old age was seen as a natural condition" (Cokayne, p.35). Physicians associated old age with phlegm and diseases linked to cold: "paralysis, numbness, tremor, convulsions, mucus, sore throats" (p. 37). They described urinary, respiratory, and kidney ailments as common in advanced age. Women were considered to age faster than men, with the menopause a more abrupt transition than any experienced by men (p. 38).

Patria potestas ensured the security of the male head of family who had the health to maintain it, but representations of tension between aged fathers and adult sons evoke hatred and even parricide; still, many middle-aged men will already have lost their fathers (Cokayne, pp.153–154). Romans assumed that families would take care of themselves, as there was little support for the aged outside the family. How one aged was one's own responsibility. Conflicts resulting from dementia were probably resolved privately. We don't know. Status for the aged depended upon continued ability to function; thus, disability yielded a certain marginality. But it appears that the philosophers who spoke about the importance of character knew something about the way society functioned. One's experience of aging was one's own, not something tied to old age itself. Indeed, wisdom was thought to come with study of philosophy, not the mere passage of time. Health mattered. Stories of other peoples disposing of the aged suggest that senicide was done by others and talked about by Romans.

When Cicero speaks in defiance of old age, we cannot assume he speaks for most Romans or describes a common experience. He may even be trying to convince himself. Perhaps he is putting the best possible face on one aspect of the human condition and particularly the condition of male elites. The variety of Roman sources for the history of old age reveals that health and acceptance of reality mattered. But Cicero's text would be a central one in the Renaissance, early modern, and even modern periods. He and others from the classical era provided ideas and representations that formed an important cultural heritage.

The Roman Empire spread that heritage along with roads and laws. It also provided the setting for the emergence of Christianity. We will look more closely at Christianity in the chapter on the Middle Ages, as it was one of the only sources of unity in that era, but we should note that it had ancient antecedents in Judaism and other sets of beliefs, and in many ways it represented a cultural turn away from the Roman emphasis on the body. Aging often appears less of a concern, but some of the Church Fathers whose texts were passed on through Eastern Christianity and the Coptic Christians of Egypt allowed some treatment of the old as symbols of wisdom. Western Christendom, as we will see in the next chapter, maintained some classical ideas and certainly depicted aged saints, but to the extent that it involved self-conscious departure from Jewish tradition and a rejection of Roman and Greek infatuation with the body, it often tipped the balance away from concerns for aging.

As we have seen, in various classical traditions there was greater documentation of elites than commoners and, concerning issues of authority or autonomy, richer descriptions of male experience than female. But some women's experiences were also documented, and older women in particular circumstances, widows and those with a religious calling, for example, might exercise increased autonomy. As we move ahead in time, we should be careful not to generalize too much from elite cultural sources. We have already seen differing representations and circumstances within classical civilizations themselves. European societies after the fall of Rome would not simply adhere to a unified set of classical or Christian ideas, just as South Asian societies would not be united in accepting Hindu or Muslim tradition, but classical civilizations did offer ideas and representations that would often help people experiencing historical change make sense of their lives.

Works Cited and Further Reading

Pamela T. Amoss and Stevan Harrell, eds., *Other Ways of Growing Old: Anthropological Perspectives* (Stanford: Stanford University Press, 1981).

For South Asian traditions, see Gene R. Thursby, "Islamic, Hindu, and Buddhist Conceptions of Aging," chapter 7 in *Handbook of the Humanities and Aging*, edited by Thomas R. Cole, David D. Van Tassel, and Robert Kastenbaum (NY:

Springer, 1992). For early Indian history, see Romila Thapar, *Early India: From the Origins to AD 1300* (Berkeley: University of California Press, 2002), and her very useful essay, "Ideology and the Interpretation of Early Indian History," which appears in both *Interpreting Early India* (Delhi: Oxford University Press, 1992) and *Cultural Pasts: Essays in Early Indian History* (Oxford: Oxford University Press, 2000). It warns against following colonial and early national historiography in terms of origins and racial categories (Aryan). A modern social scientific study that refers briefly to ancient Indian ideas is S. Irundaya Rajan, U.S. Mishra, P. Sankara Sarna, *India's Elderly: Burden or Challenge?* (New Delhi, Thousand Oaks, London: Sage, 1999); for a less idealized view, see Albrecht Wezler, "Old Age and the Elderly in Ancient and Mediaeval India," in Susanne Formanek and Sepp Linhart, eds., *Aging: Asian Concepts and Experiences, Past and Present* (Vienna: Verlag der Österreichischen Akademie der Wissenschaften, 1997), pp. 37–63; Kenneth G. Zysk, *Asceticism and Healing in Ancient India: Medicine in the Buddhist Monastery* (NY and Oxford: Oxford University Press, 1991); A.L. Basham, "The Practice of Medicine in Ancient and Medieval India," in *Asian Medical Systems: A Comparative Study*, edited by Charles Leslie (Berkeley: University of California Press, 1976); *The Roots of Ayurveda: Selections from Sanskrit Medical Writings*, selected, translated, and edited by Dominik Wujastyk (New Delhi, London, NY: Penguin Books, 1998); Dagmar Benner, "Healing and Medicine: Healing and Medicine in Ayurveda and South Asia," in *Encyclopedia of Religion*, 2nd edition, edited by Lindsay Jones (NY: MacMillan, 2005): 3852–3858; Nongluck Pussayapibul, Samrit Srithamrongsawat, and Kanitta Bundhamcharoen, "Ageing in Thailand: Challenges and Policy Responses," in Tsung-hsi Fu and Rhidian Hughes, eds., *Ageing in East Asia: Challenges and Policies for the Twenty-First Century* (London and NY: Routledge, 2009), p. 167.

For Chinese traditions, see Charlotte Ikels, ed., *Filial Piety: Practice and Discourse in Contemporary East Asia* (Stanford: Stanford University Press, 2004); François Jullien, "Vieillesse et longévité: comment penser le procès de la vie?," in Maurice Godelier, François Jullien, and Joseph Maïla, *Le grand âge de la vie* (Paris: PUF, 2005). Lines from Confucius, *Analects*, as excerpted in *The Oxford Book of Aging: Reflections on the Journey of Life*, edited by Thomas R. Cole and Mary G. Winkler (Oxford and NY: OUP, 1994): 26–27; Wang Ch'ung, *Lun heng*, Part I, *Philosophical Essays of Wang Ch'ung*, Alfred Forke, translator (Shanghai: Kelly and Walsh, 1907); Mencius, *The Chinese Classics*, Volume II: *The Works of Mencius*, translated by James Legge (Oxford: Clarendon Press, 1895); James Legge, translator, *The Sacred Books of China*, Part III: *The Li Ki*, I-X, in Frank Müller, editor, *The Sacred Books of the East*, Vol. 27, and *The Sacred Books of China*, Part IV, *The Li Ki*, XI-XLVI, in Frank Müller, editor, *The Sacred Books of the East*, Volume 28 (Oxford: Oxford University Press, 1885). The classic texts can be found online thanks to the Chinese Text Project: http://ctext.org. Simone de Beauvoir, *La vieillesse* (Paris: Gallimard, 1970), English translation *The Coming of Age* (NY: Putnam, 1972). On the Chinese family, see Michel Cartier, "China: the Family as a Relay of Government," in *A History of the Family*, Vol. I, *Distant Worlds, Ancient Worlds*, edited by André Burguière, Christiane Klapisch-Zuber, Martine Segalen, and Françoise Zonabend (Cambridge: Harvard University Press, 1996).

On Mesopotamia, see Jean-Jacques Glassner, "From Sumer to Babylon: Families as Landowners and Families as Rulers," in *A History of the Family*; Rivkah Harris, *Gender and Aging in Mesopotamia: The Gilgamesh Epic and Other Ancient Literature* (Norman: University of Oklahoma Press, 2000). On Egypt, see Annie Forgeau, "The Survival of the Family Name and the Pharaonic Order," in *A History of the Family*; Jac. J. Janssen and Rosalind M. Janssen, *Getting Old in Ancient Egypt* (London: Rubicon, 1996). On the Hebrews, see Harold M. Stahmer, "The Aged in Two Ancient Oral Cultures: The Ancient Hebrews and Homeric Greece," in *Aging and the Elderly: Humanistic Perspectives in Gerontology*, edited by Stuart F. Spicker, Kathleen M. Woodward, David D. Van Tassel (Atlantic Highlands, NJ: Humanities Press, 1978); Sheldon Isenberg, "Aging in Judaism: 'Crown of Glory' and 'Days of Sorrow,'" chapter 6 in *Handbook of the Humanities and Aging*.

Among the many works concerning Greece and Rome, see the pertinent chapters in Georges Minois, *History of Old Age: from Antiquity to the Renaissance* (Chicago: University of Chicago Press, 1989); Ennio Bauer, "Old Age as a Principle of Social Organization: *Gerousiai* in the *Poleis* of Hellenistic and Roman Southern Asia Minor," in *On Old Age: Approaching Death in Antiquity and the Middle Ages*, edited by Christian Krötzl and Katariina Mustakallio (Turnhout: Brepols, 2011), pp. 127–152; Tim Parkin, "The Ancient Greek and Roman Worlds," in Pat Thane, ed., *A History of Old Age* (London: Thames and Hudson, 2005); Thomas M. Falkner and Judith de Luce, "A View from Antiquity: Greece, Rome, and Elders," in *Handbook of the Humanities and Aging*; Karen Cokayne, *Experiencing Old Age in Ancient Rome* (London: Routledge, 2003). On Greece in particular, see Bessie Richardson's *Old Age among the Ancient Greeks: The Greek Portrayal of Old Age in Literature, Art and Inscriptions* (Baltimore: Johns Hopkins University Press, 1933); Andrée Catrysse, *Les grecs et la vieillesse, d'Homère à Epicure* (Paris: L'Harmattan, 2003). On Rome, see Tim Parkin, *Old Age in the Roman World: A Cultural and Social History* (Baltimore: Johns Hopkins University Press, 2003); Mary Harlow and Ray Laurence, "Viewing the Old: Recording and Respecting the Elderly at Rome and in the Empire," in Krötzl and Mustakallio, pp. 3–23; Aleksandr Koptev, "The Massacre of Old Men by the Gauls in 390 B.C. and the Social Meaning of Old Age in Early Rome," in Krötzl and Mustakallio, pp. 153–182; Katariina Mustakallio, "Representing Older Women: Hersilia, Veturia, Virgo Vestalis Maxima," in Krötzl and Mustakallio, pp. 41–56. On the Copts: Sydney H. Aufrère and Nathalie Bosson, "La vieillesse et la hiérarchie des anciens," in *D'âge en âge* (Paris: L'Harmattan, 2008).

SECTION II
Medieval to Early Modern Transformations

4

AGING IN THE MIDDLE AGES AND THE RENAISSANCE

A Western focus leads one to think about the Middle Ages as a period of collapse of political institutions, dramatic decentralization, and the emergence of Christianity as, along with the Latin language, the only thing tying Europe together. We will explore the impact of such trends on aging and the aged. But we will also look at how some of the themes of the classical civilizations discussed in chapter 3 were taken up elsewhere and developed in subsequent centuries. Thus, Islam built upon and departed from Jewish and Christian ideas and practices, and Chinese culture spread to diverse populations in East Asia. All had something to say about aging and the aged. As we did in the last chapter, let us begin in the East and work our way West.

A look at China reveals the maintenance of Confucian ideas. T'ang legal codes enshrined the Confucian emphasis on patriarchy for centuries after that dynasty had fallen. Indeed, historians see the tradition continuing until the end of the Qing Dynasty in 1912. "The legal power of the elderly tended to gain strength as it was incorporated into classical Chinese culture, especially features of kinship groups and kinship-based magico-religious beliefs about fate, death, and the afterlife" (Kiefer, p. 98). Lineage became important in joining together related households looking back at a common ancestor. Between 1000 and 1300 CE, one would have found large numbers of relatives collaborating on the tracing of ancestry across multiple generations (p. 99). Lineage solidarity and ancestor worship were central to the maintenance of Confucian ritual and the authority of older men. Where tradition was followed, the aged were honored in the family and exercised economic authority. In a culture characterized by ancestor worship, even death did not interrupt the attention one deserved and received. At least that's the ideal. The historical record tells us little about the degree to which the weakened aged in the real world could count on the support that Chinese thought mandated, and scholars have begun to nuance the "traditional respect" view of Asian aging.

Confucianism spread throughout East Asia. Scholars see an intensification of Confucian patriarchy in Korea even beyond what existed in much of China (p. 108). Korea resembled China in being patriarchal and patrilineal, but inheritance and household patterns differed, with primogeniture operating in Korea and shared inheritance among the Chinese. Such sharing would become moot in the one-child family of contemporary China.

The period we think of as medieval in Europe is a period of great Chinese influence in Japan, especially from the sixth to ninth centuries CE. Confucian ideas supporting hierarchy, reverence for the aged, and ritual played a major role in Japan. Japanese social organization, with its notion of responsibility to the collectivity, would ideally have accorded important status and protection for the aged. And it's possible to speak of a feudal order in Japan to parallel that in Europe. But it is extremely hard to historicize actual practice when the scholarly literature posits long-term continuity and points out great distinctions between public and private behavior. For example, Kiefer writes: "In a formalistic society with strong Confucian elements … the aged, especially men, received respect and obedience in public but in private often deferred to more capable subordinates" (p. 114). One wonders whether in the cases of elders who did not so defer, Confucian ideals of respect might have been sorely tested. One wonders, too, how far back in time one can go and still apply the following observation by Kiefer:

> It is not so much that the aged were revered as that one's character was likely to be measured by one's compassion for them, especially the sick, and the frail. To neglect, mistreat, or ignore one's elders was more than a breach of manners; it was a sign of defective character. Of course, the aged themselves would be judged by their compassion for the young.
>
> *(p. 115)*

Some students of Japanese culture see great ambiguity and even cruelty and abandonment in Japanese ways of dealing with the aged—the most extreme expression comes from a Japanese folktale called *Obasuteyama* ("Throw-Out-Granny Mountain")—but in terms of modern uses of traditional cultures, ideals are ideals, and they often accentuate the positive.

In thinking about respect for and treatment of the aged around the world, it is tempting to see parallels between virtually all of the major civilizations and religions. Confucians in East Asia, Hindus in South Asia, and Hebrews in the Middle East all showed respect for the aged. The same can be said of Muslims. Hebrew patriarchs themselves reappear in the Quran. Both there (15:54) and in the Hebrew Bible, Abraham and Sara learn that they will be parents in old age. The Quran presents old age as a sign of mortality, a sign that one should think of eternity. Yet, as one scholar puts it, "In the Qur'an the elderly receive far less attention than the young" and passages referring to old age expressed a considerable amount of revulsion, focusing on the inability to have children, physical weakness, and a generally pitiable condition (O'Shaughnessy, p. 45). Scholars of the Quran suggest that the pre-Islamic Arabic world was characterized by attitudes of respect for the aged and that the emergence of Islam involved a decided preference for youth, as the religious knowledge of Muhammad's own youthful followers trumped any idea of respect for seniority.

The Hadith (Sayings of Muhammad) offer a range of ideas, including the linkage of age with death and encouragement to think not of worldly things. Thus, "The grave is the first stage of the journey into eternity," "Death is a bridge that uniteth friend with friend," and "Love of this world is the chief of all errors." The prayers of the aged are said to be particularly welcome, and calls for filial piety are addressed to the young. "If it were not for your elderly folk with their bent backs, calamities would have descended on you in floods." "To every young person who honoureth the old, on account of their age, may God appoint those who shall honour him in his years. Verily, to honour an old man is showing respect to God." The Hadith, like classical texts from around the ancient world, contrast youth and age. "The best of the youths among you are those who imitate those of mature years, while the worst of your elderly are those who imitate the young." Of course, the essential context is that of showing submission to Allah at all ages. But the eventual ravages of age might make the point even more forcefully. Frailty and dependence are to be contrasted with divine power.

Medieval poetry from the Islamic world offers reflections on physical decline, change, and mortality, as in a tenth-century lament by Rudaki or the thirteenth-century writings of Rumi (*Oxford Book of Aging*, pp. 312 and 98). The first major study of the theme of age in Arabic literature describes the dualities of youth and age in medieval poetry and other genres. It identifies poetic imagery of the black raven and the white falcon that represented youth and old age (*al-shabab va-l-shayb*). Black hair was seen as beautiful, gray hair (*shayb*) as abhorrent. Even though gray or white hair could sometimes symbolize dignity and filial piety was presented as trumping military jihad, "the obsession with gray hair is peculiar to Arabic literature" (Shuraydi, p. 9) and decidedly negative. As had happened in Christianity, a movement seeking to distance itself from its origins (Judaism in the Christian case) privileged youth over age. An Islamic tradition, distinguishing itself from both Judaism and Christianity, urged Muslim men to dye their hair to maintain the black, youthful ideal. By contrast, women engaging in the practice were subject to mockery, at least according to Arabic literature.

It is difficult to say how literary representations compare to historical experience of individuals and families, but one scholar of medieval Islam, Thierry Bianquis, has provided an overview of the medieval Arab family. He points out that poetry expresses extremes and historical accounts discuss the public lives of notables, but that legal writings can complement sacred and poetic ones. The big challenge to the family was to maintain its long-term economic viability, to protect it from the political power of a given moment. Marital practices, including polygamy, functioned to guarantee maintenance and growth of population in a harsh environment. As far as the elderly were concerned, a couple of features of the medieval family are worth noting. The ease with which husbands could repudiate wives might well have put aging women at risk; yet, the difference in age between husbands (marrying right up to old age) and wives (marrying soon after puberty) seemed to mitigate the danger. The age difference was thought to have made the husband more distant to wives and children (a phenomenon also observed in Renaissance Florence), but the attachment between mother and children could also protect wives from the risk of repudiation (Bianquis, p. 44). Naming practices by which an eldest son often received the first name (*ism*) of his grandfather suggest the importance of lineage as does the shift in a new father's designation (*kunya*) from "son of" to "father of." Those who had wealth and status could eventually achieve the rank of *sheikh* or "noble old man." Family and wealth ensured continued comfort, but those who couldn't guarantee their own subsistence and had no children encountered a difficult old age. Some of the men who never married formed gangs of youth, upsetting the social order, but some may have been welcomed by the wives of aged merchants (p. 47).

How Muslim ideas as related to old age interacted with other ideas in a late medieval world characterized by important trade networks in both the Indian Ocean and the Mediterranean Sea is largely unknown. Historians have made progress in tracing commercial routes for the exchange of goods, and art historians have identified influences in style and technique, but virtually the only area where modern scholarship has described the transmission of non-religious ideas about aging is in science and medicine. Much of that involved the preservation and communication of Greek texts. Bedouins had inherited some practices from the pre-Islamic period of "tribal leaders and old women" (Rahman, p. 33), but the humoral medicine that was so central in the Mediterranean world was picked up by Muslim physicians from North Africa to India, and influences ran between Greek, Persian, and Indian medical thought. Medicine was one important part of the philosophy of Al Tabari and Al Razi in the ninth and tenth centuries and above all Avicenna (980–1037), who preserved the medicine of the Greeks, speaking of loss of innate moisture and heat.

Medical historians have begun to detect change over the course of centuries, but continuity seems to be the greater theme. Knowledge of pharmacology remained important, and some developments in surgery have been noted, but the language of medicine hardly changed, and it would be difficult to claim any important change in the understanding of advanced age. Continuity appears to be the rule in the world of Islamic thought about aging, but there has been very little work on the subject. Fortunately, one of the most influential Islamic thinkers of the twentieth century, Said Nursi, wrote a treatise on old age which recent scholarship presents as both embodying tradition and illustrating the particular context in which he lived and worked. Nursi (1877–1960) was a Kurdish Muslim in Anatolia who wrote primarily in Ottoman Turkish but also in Arabic. In the last decades of the Ottoman Empire, he favored religious reform, and in the period of the

First World War and the founding of the modern Turkish state he found himself at an important crossroads. He long encouraged the teaching of both science and religion and opposed the more radical secularizing policies of the state. He spent many years in exile or in prison (including as a prisoner of war in Russia during the First World War), and after a profound spiritual experience in the aftermath of the war and the revolutionary changes brought forth by Turkish modernizers, he turned inward (from the "old" Said to the "new" Said) and devoted himself to a massive commentary called the *Risale-i Nur*. This included his so-called *Flashes*, composed in the 1930s but looking back to the crucial years of the war and the early 1920s. Among these texts was a "Treatise on Old Age." Because the central theme of the work was the importance of the Quran, and because of influences that included several strands of medieval Islamic thought, we can think of it as offering an important vision of the Islamic tradition while also being the product of a particular historical moment.

Just as Cicero had intended his *De Senectute* as a refutation of common objections to old age, so Nursi's text sought to counter the "sorrows and afflictions" of old age. He found his solution in the words of the "All-Wise Quran": "Infirm indeed are my bones, and the hair of my head glistens with grey; but I am never unblest, O my Sustainer, in my prayer to you" (19:1–4). He recounted his experience at around the age of 40:

> One day as I was entering upon old age, in the autumn at the time of the afternoon prayer, I was gazing on the world from a high mountain. Suddenly I was overwhelmed by a plaintive, sorrowful and in one respect dark state of mind. I saw that I had become old. The day too had grown old, and so had the year; so too had the world become old. As the time of departure from the world and separation from those I loved was drawing close within these instances of old age, my own old age shook me severely. Suddenly divine mercy unfolded in such a way that it transformed that plaintive sadness and separation into a powerful hope and shining light of solace.
> *("The Twenty-Sixth Flash," in* The Flashes Collection*, p. 286)*

Thus, divine mercy as embodied in the Quran transforms sadness into hope. He used as a metaphor for the aging body the gradual collapse of a building, an approach found in the Hebrew Prophets, and described a world that itself, in the wake of world war and the demise of empires and the caliphate, had reached old age. As fall gave way to winter, the entire landscape, both natural and built, including a cemetery viewed from atop a mountain, bespeaks sorrow, but the light of the Quran breaks through the darkness.

The many volumes of the *Risale-i Nur* have gained him many followers, particularly in Turkey, and recent scholars praise his voice of moderation, spiritualism, and pacifism, but he had his detractors, who sometimes saw him as speaking more narrowly for his fellow Kurds. Yet, his writings, while influenced by centuries of Islamic thought, emphasize above all the reading of the Quran, and his treatise, in the absence of other texts on old age, may be taken as representing more than just one individual's work. Still, it should be kept in mind that modern literature of the Islamic world does not always adhere to religious principles. Thus, one study of modern Arabic literature has virtually nothing to say about religious representations of old age but emphasizes lyrical evocations of the passage of time, and Islam Ahmad El Said, an Egyptian graffiti artist in the second decade of the twenty-first century, creates an aged character, Am BulBul, to speak truth to power because he claims that, regardless of ideology, modern Egypt still respects old age and even allows it to speak crudely.

The Islamic tradition had, among other things, built upon Christianity and considered Jesus one of the prophets in the line extending to Muhammad, but Christian ideas represented a departure from both the pagan and Jewish pasts. For the elderly, this has sometimes been characterized as unfortunate. Christianity self-consciously saw itself as abandoning old ways of thinking. Just as it was common to distinguish between the Jewish "Old" Testament and the Christian "New" one, so Christian religious practice involved a rhetoric of rebirth and renewal. The emphasis on spirituality involved a turn away from, if not renunciation of, the body. The pains of aging could be viewed as a distraction from what was most important, the business of salvation.

Christian tradition, whether in the writings of the Church fathers or in centuries of sermon literature, used old age as a metaphor. Old age represented the body and sinfulness; youth represented the soul and salvation. The punishment for Original Sin was mortality and the process of aging. Theologians encouraged contempt for the flesh, the self, and the world (*contemptus mundi*). Vanity is the great enemy. But even though the development of Christian spirituality involved a turn away from classical precedent, the religious Middle Ages did not just abandon classical learning. Medieval authors described the life course (*cursus aetatis*) in ways that hearkened back to antiquity, most commonly dividing a life into three, four, six, or seven stages. According to John Burrow, biologists saw three ages, physiologists four, and astrologers seven. Saint Augustine chose six stages in *On Genesis against the Manichees* (388–390). This corresponded to the six days of creation, and Elizabeth Sears argues that Isidore of Seville (d. 636), Bede, and Hrabanus Maurus (840s) followed suit. Individual ages differed in duration, but multiples of seven were popular, and for centuries women reached a critical period (menopause) at 49, while men might have reached a critical moment at 63 and definitive old age at 70. The terms used to identify the later ages came right out of the classical past: *gravitas, senectus, senium,* or *decrepitas*. And the idea of the ages of life had roots we have already seen in Mesopotamia and Egypt.

Medievalist Shulamith Shahar, in writing on old age, connects classical and medieval thinking. She describes how Vincent of Beauvais (c. 1190–1264) followed Maximianus in treating old age, evoking the "smell of death" and "death in life" (Shahar, "Old Age in the High and Late Middle Ages," p. 45). And she demonstrates how Innocent III (1160–1216) borrowed from Horace on the old man's body:

> his heart weakens and his head shakes; his face becomes wrinkled and his back becomes bent; his eyes grow dim and his joints grow shaky; his nose runs and his hair falls out; his hand trembles and he makes awkward movements; his teeth decay and his ears grow deaf. And he adds: 'young men! be not proud in the presence of a decaying old man; he was once that which you are; he is now what you in turn will be'.
>
> *(p. 46)*

Shahar claims that for Innocent old age "symbolizes the terrible judgement in the next world which man in his folly and sin chooses to ignore" (Ibid.).

Just as classical representations of the old woman evoked disgust, medieval thinkers aimed for the same reaction by offering her as a symbol of sin.

> In *Le Pèlerinage de la vie humaine*, written in the fourteenth century by William of Deguileville, the different virtues like Mercy, Charity, Reason, Penitence and Diligence...as well as God's Grace are personified by young women splendidly dressed. While Sloth, Pride, Flattery, Hypocrisy, Envy, Treachery, Anger, Avarice, Gluttony and Lust, as well as Tribulation, Heresy, Disease and Old Age, are represented by ugly old women. Sloth is an ugly, hairy, dirty and stinking old woman. Pride is an old woman of monstrous obesity...
>
> *(p. 47)*

Classical philosophy on aging could make its way into the literature on the education of princes. Aegidius Romanus (ca. 1247–1316) wrote such a manual for his pupil, the future King Philip the Fair of France. We hear echoes of Aristotle in the list of negative characteristics: "cowardly, suspicious, shameless (because advantage is more important to them than honour), miserly and lacking in hope" (p. 49).

Moralists warned against complaint. Acceptance and resignation were encouraged. Shahar quotes Bernardino of Siena, addressing the complaining elder: "You strove to reach it [old age], and you desired to achieve it, you were afraid you'll not reach it, now, arriving, you lament. Every one wishes to reach old age, but nobody wishes to be old" (p. 50).

One needn't have been a scholar or even literate to have encountered representations of the ages of life or of old age. True, illuminated manuscripts were rather specialized items, but stained glass windows, sculptures, and murals were there for all to see. Often in the late Middle Ages the ages of life were represented in cyclical or serial form: the wheel of life or tree of life. Even though we can see ages represented differently, one of the important messages was that at every age one must be prepared to meet death. Earthly life was characterized by human vanity, a sin that was supposedly accentuated in old age.

Medieval epic literature tended to focus attention on youth and strength, including military accomplishment, but science, moral philosophy, and popular literature continued to discuss advanced age in the late Middle Ages. Galenic medical thought was built upon by Arab physician Avicenna (980–1037), who explained individual aging through such factors as climate, nutrition, and exercise. Such ideas influenced Roger Bacon (d. 1290s) and Arnald of Villanova (d. 1311), who sought ways of slowing or even preventing the aging process. In the 1280s, Bacon expressed considerable optimism in *The Cure of Old Age and the Preservation of Youth*. He offered advice for healthy living but observed an environmental challenge: the increasing number of people and animals inhabiting the earth were a source of pollution. Arnald further developed Bacon's approach and added a large dose of mysticism in *The Defence of Age and Recovery of Youth*. In a less elevated vein, old age in Romance is presented as shrunken, feeble, and ugly, and popular tales are filled with lascivious and avaricious crones, reminiscent of the cruelest representations in Roman comedy.

Moving from the world of high and popular culture to more social historical sources, we find a serious devaluing of old age. In a violent era, youth had its privileges, and death in battle was certainly more heroic than death from old age. "Customary law assessing damages for wrongful death shows us an old person valued as the equal of a child under the age of 10. Germanic codes also indicate a relatively early end to a father's control over his children (Mitterauer and Sieder). This was a far cry from Roman patriarchy. For non-elites, old age must have implied a significant loss of power. Nevertheless, some evidence suggests a popular association between age and the supernatural, particularly old women whose experience with birth, disease, and death placed them at the margin of the natural and the magical" (Troyansky, "The Older Person in the Western World," p. 44). Still, not all midwives or accused witches in late medieval or early modern Europe were aged, and many old women wielded no such authority.

The idea of old age was linked to qualities and function, not often to chronological age. Popes tended to be middle-aged and old, elected between their 50s and 70s and serving almost always for life. Many other church officials remained in their positions well into old age. Kings were somewhat younger, and nobles, especially in their military roles, were often subject to early death. The administrative life that would become more common in the early modern era held out the promise of greater life expectancy. Kings and feudal lords, of course, could force others to retire.

In the decentralized, ruder world of the Middle Ages, state structures were less well developed than they had been in ancient Rome, but we do have records of what constituted public life, and some called for age awareness. Exemptions from military service, local administrative tasks, and payment of certain taxes existed, and unsurprisingly the ages of 60 and 70 were often the key moments. The 1349 Statute of Labourers in England required men and women only up to 60 to accept work offered to them. In the Crusader Kingdom of Jerusalem an heiress of a fief at age 60 could resist a lord's order to marry (Shahar, "Old Age in the High and Late Middle Ages," p. 43).

Exemption hardly meant forced inactivity or retirement, but individual decisions included the possibility of withdrawing from active life. As Joel Rosenthal puts it,

> We can look back and say that retirement was an idea in search of a structure on which to rest: personal wealth, community charity, or some idea of institutional commitment and subsidization, as with some fortunate clerics and some select groups of civil and royal servants, might make it possible. But at best it was applied on a limited and sporadic basis.
>
> *(p. 100)*

Evidence from the House of Lords indicates that some older members excused themselves from attendance in the spirit of putting a "reasonable interval" before death (p. 126). "Neither continuing participation, nor retirement and withdrawal, can be termed the characteristic behavior. Neither is there much to support any idea that these men and women turned to religion and religious activity" (p. 134).

Shahar offers greater support for the idea of aging individuals seeking religious retreat and opportunities for contemplation in advanced age, and Minois sees wealthy elders beginning to retire to monasteries as early as the sixth century. In effect, they were breaking from the world in a more dramatic fashion than did the elders of the Roman patriciate. By the eleventh century, it had become more common, with some elders residing with younger monks and others living separately, but all engaged in contemplative retreat. Marie-Thérèse Lorcin finds widows entering monasteries and lay religious communities. In some cases, widows made financial donations in return for support in communities. By the thirteenth century in France, they made such arrangements with hospitals. Even if such institutions left overall control to men (doctors for hospitals, the church hierarchy for religious communities), everyday authority could fall to women. Thus, there were settings in which some women might exercise considerable autonomy and do so into advanced age.

For men who had made a career of religious activity, one took time to reach the top as a bishop and then sometimes resigned with a pension in advanced age. Of course, in pre-Reformation Europe, the celibate clergy required institutional support that others might have received from children. Monastic life offered communal support, and such support, including food and shelter, may actually have increased life expectancy among the religious of both sexes. And if women were in a position to avoid pregnancy altogether, they could avoid serious health risks in medieval conditions.

In contrast to monastic clergy, secular clergy lived active lives in the world. One recent study demonstrates that most did not in late life use a monastery as a retirement home, but it does provide examples of retirement arrangements involving resignation of a benefice, turning it over to a successor, and receiving an annual pension (Kirsi Salonen, p. 187). The author finds the occasional aged bishop resigning from a diocese or having to co-exist with a co-bishop appointed in case of disability. But this was the exception, as ordination was a life-long commitment.

Shahar found examples of pensions delivered within institutions and others, especially in the late Middle Ages, paid by individuals at home. She describes how urban guilds throughout Europe began working out arrangements that would, in a later period, be characteristic of benevolent societies. But of course most Europeans in the Middle Ages, and well into the nineteenth century, lived in the countryside, and rural aging took on a variety of forms. We have already mentioned that feudal lords could force the unproductive into retirement, but feudalism was not characteristic of the entire continent, and it would be greatly weakened in the West by the Black Death in the fourteenth century. For the most part, the generations worked out their own transitions according to custom and experience. Shahar describes two models of peasant retirement, one in which the head of the household remains officially in place but makes promises about the future, the other in which authority is transferred. Transfer became more common following the Black Death, as aging peasants established the next generation and assured their own support contractually. When Shakespeare dramatized the dangers of premortem transmission of property and authority and the intergenerational sentiment that accompanied succession in *King Lear*, he was borrowing from earlier literary models but also from everyday practice that characterized peasants as well as royalty. Lear's predicament was easily understood in a world in which land was the greatest form of wealth.

Countless numbers of medieval wills anticipated the early modern practice of notarizing maintenance contracts in families of peasants and artisans. In some parts of the European countryside, we assume that few property owners passed on their holdings before physical debility encouraged retirement; at least there was plenty of advice, both written and oral, to warn against putting oneself at risk, and notarized contracts demonstrate the result of negotiations between generations. For every written contract, there must have been plenty of cases of informal agreement. The elder's authority might even outlive him (or more rarely her), as testaments might dictate particular long-term arrangements from the grave.

High death rates, especially when accompanied by delayed marriage, precluded lengthy coexistence of two adult generations. But by the late twelfth century, Georges Duby finds such coexistence and even what he describes as a generation gap. Rosenthal sees three-generation families as not too unusual in England in the late Middle Ages.

Although the majority of the medieval population was rural and generations found themselves negotiating over land, we must recognize the importance of commercial cities in the late Middle Ages. Business classes had their comparable experience of succession and possible retirement in the context of economic expansion and urban growth. Wealth and longevity would have encouraged secular retirement, and urban institutions were beginning to provide some opportunities for lifetime annuity arrangements.

After centuries of growth, the Black Death of the fourteenth century had a major impact on European society and culture. Some historians see a new worldliness; others, a revived religiosity. Much depends upon the location and source. Some Italian populations have been relatively well studied, and historians have revealed that younger people were disproportionately represented among plague victims; the result was a significant aging of some populations. Ten percent of the Tuscan peasantry was over 65 years of age in 1427, 11% of the working class and lower middle class. A prescriptive literature on family life emerged in the wake of the plague. It called for respect for aged parents, but whether it did anything more than prescribe proper behavior is difficult to say. What we do know is that emerging marriage patterns involved an important age gap between husbands and wives. The "old man," therefore, was more likely a husband and father rather than grandfather, but we would need more demographic data from other parts of Europe to know whether Tuscany was exceptional.

What was true both in Tuscany and elsewhere was the importance of widowhood, which was not primarily an experience of the aged. High mortality rates meant high rates of widowhood, but men were much more likely than women to remarry and to do so quickly. Historians of medieval and early modern Europe have applied the term "city of widows" to several locations. For women, widowhood could be a long-lasting state, one within which advanced age might eventually be reached. In many cases, this meant vulnerability. Among substantial landowners and urban middle classes, however, widows could enjoy considerable autonomy right up to old age. Depending upon location, they might inherit something of the legal status and control of property that their late husbands had enjoyed. They exercised responsibility over matters of family strategy. Widowhood changed women's status. Men's legal status remained the same, but their rush to remarry may tell us of their own sense of vulnerability as much as it tells us of their privilege. Historians have described the lot of aristocratic, middle-class, and artisanal widowhood in the Middle Ages and through the early modern period. Janine Lanza, who has written about widows in the world of Parisian crafts, is one among several historians who describe them as "honorary men," exercising authority in family and community. She suggests a decline in status that came with legal changes in the era of the French Revolution.

Prescriptive, literary, and legal sources reveal different aspects of widowhood, whether recommendations of religious devotion, depictions of uncontrolled sexuality, or contractual relations. The same can be said for ways of representing anticipations of death. Boccaccio's *Decameron*, in which people in hiding from the plague entertain each other with stories, reveals one reaction to demographic crisis; testamentary practices may reveal something else. In testaments from Siena, for example, a new strategy for the afterlife and pious earthly bequests emerges in the late fourteenth and early fifteenth centuries, and a certain selfishness becomes evident in the late fifteenth and sixteenth centuries. Eventually, the Counter-Reformation would encourage a new kind of piety, which would decline only in the eighteenth century.

Shahar examines the role of age in late medieval cities and contrasts what happened in Lucca and in Venice. "The only case of legal disqualification from office due to chronological age I encountered is in the statutes of Lucca. People aged 55 and over could not be elected to public offices." Elsewhere there were exemptions and a right to retire if one chose. Venice was at the opposite extreme from Lucca. There it was closer to a gerontocracy.

> Only old men (in their sixties, seventies and sometimes even in their eighties) were elected to the office of doge, and the election was for life. Very rarely was a man under 50 elected to the ruling councils like the Senate, The Council of Ten and the Collegio. The power of the elderly patricians who ruled Venice was based on a combination of the 'ascriptive' criterion of age and an 'achieved' criterion.

But Lucca and Venice were exceptions. "In general no preference was given to the elderly on the one hand, nor were they obliged to retire so long as their functional capacity did not fail, on the other hand" (Shahar, "Old Age in the High and Late Middle Ages", pp. 54–55). Those who weren't well off kept working as long as possible. Laborers would work until no one would hire them.

A study of old age in medieval towns in Hungary notes that there were no baptismal or death records before the end of the sixteenth century, so there wasn't much age consciousness. Still, the arrival of old age could be identified by physical signs and obvious disability (Szende, p. 201). Where support was needed, a range of solutions was found. In a sample of about 1,300 late medieval wills from three Hungarian towns, 79 (6%) mentioned living parents, and individual testaments called for provision for an aged parent. One such testament, written in German in November 1467, declared:

> I order that my father, Andre, has to be taken care of beside my son Wolfgang, and be provided with food and clothes as long as he lives in a proper way from my bequest. Should he, however, be impatient and unbearable because of his impatience, he has to be given a pension fund according to the council of the executors of my testament and of further honourable pensions. …But I want that my father be taken care of in any case, as it was written above.
>
> (p. 203)

Care of a mother-in-law is spelled out in her son's 1481 will in Pressburg:

> I leave to my wife that she should keep my mother with her and feed her as long as she lives, as I trust her [the wife]. Should it happen, however, that the two

of them cannot stand each other, then I leave to my mother one of my vineyards named Perg by St Nicholas church as long as she lives...

(p. 204)

Of course, remarriage could serve a needy surviving spouse.

There was little institutionalized retirement in east central Europe before the thirteenth century, but there may well have been informal arrangements. Individuals could co-reside. Some nobles chose to move into religious institutions, but it was hardly a common solution. Hospitals might serve the aged, along with the poor and infirm, but they weren't very numerous in eastern Europe. They were more common in western and central Europe, and in most cases can be seen as linked to religious foundations.

In the typical survey of European history, the Renaissance follows upon the Middle Ages, but a traditional way of seeing Renaissance individualism as constituting something completely unprecedented has given way to a tendency to embed the Renaissance in a largely medieval world. To speak about any theme in the Renaissance is to focus attention on cultural representations that revived ancient thought, and it becomes a question of what strand of ancient culture was being revived. For Georges Minois, who saw the ancients as railing against old age, the Renaissance would not offer a cheerful picture. "By re-establishing its links with ancient Greece, the Renaissance instinctively rediscovered the Hellenes' horror of old age" (Minois, p. 249). For him it was a literary and courtly cult of youth that marginalized old age. Others, however, point to a cultural world that appreciated the aged physiognomy, created a diversity of elderly literary characters, and revived and developed ancient prescriptive literature that fought disability and decrepitude. Scholars investigating how Renaissance writers represented the ages of life, the aging body, and ways of living in advanced age find Minois' view too pessimistic (Winn and Yandell; Campbell).

When looking at literary sources from the Renaissance and after we need to keep in mind that writers were adapting earlier models of character and plot rather than simply representing their own era. English literary representations even in the seventeenth century built upon classical, medieval, and Renaissance Italian models. One recent study looks precisely at Italian influence on English dramatic depiction of the elderly by such writers as Shakespeare, Jonson, and Dekker. Galenic medicine, Italian writings on longevity, and *commedia dell'arte* depictions of the elderly made their way across the English Channel from the European continent. Themes of gerontocracy and intergenerational conflict were portrayed in both Italy and England.

Shakespeare transformed earlier themes and representations into the works that would serve as literary touchstones forever after. Thus, King Lear would arguably be the most important representation of old age for centuries and draw the attention of philosophers of aging in the twenty-first century. But Shakespeare peopled his plays with an extraordinary diversity of old characters: wise men and fools, jealous men and statesmen; strong, loving, and lusty old women. His famous version of the "Ages of Man" in *As You Like It* is only one of his representations of what it meant to grow old (even in that one play).

Renaissance and post-Renaissance painting is just beginning to be studied for its representations of old age. As in textual representation, pictorial images need to be read carefully. Portraits survive of saints and heroes, political officials and humanist scholars. They range between obviously idealized sacred and profane characters, somewhat more realistic, if also somewhat idealized, likenesses of notable individuals, and embodiments of decline and decay. A walk through any major museum of European art offers representations of aged individuals. Breughel the Elder depicted decrepit elders. Albrecht Dürer portrayed his mother in an enigmatic way that for some betrays despair and for others represents an allegory of the passage of time. Art historians have described a sense of calm in Raphael's work and great intensity in Tintoretto's. It is easy to see affection in the gazes of Ghirlandaio's old man and young boy, but we can't assume they represent grandfather and grandson. Effigies that depict elderly royals or portraits of wealthy and accomplished elders by such artists as Jan Van Eyck and Filippo Lippi are hardly representative of "typical" old persons, although one might argue that Michelangelo's elders embody a strength of character that transcends social station.

Caroline Schuster Cardone has devoted a book to images of female old age from the late fifteenth century to the seventeenth. The themes that emerge are the relationship of the old woman to society and family, depictions of the aged body, and attitudes toward sexuality in advanced age and late maternity. What she finds is the development of an iconography of female old age in the sixteenth century and a process of diversification in the seventeenth. Renaissance portraiture stood at the beginning of a tradition of representation of the individual, but cultural norms concerning the female body and its decline shaped images of pious and somewhat "masculinized" older women. They moralized about late pregnancy and nursing as either miraculous or transgressive, and they used the old woman as grotesque embodiment of vanity and out-of-control sexuality but also as representation of piety, motherhood, and mature advice-giving.

Old age as metaphor became more systematized in Ripa's *Iconologia* in the late sixteenth and seventeenth centuries. Such representations built upon themes found in classical and medieval representations and taught aspiring artists the rules of the game. Again virtue tended to be young, vice old, but portrayals of the ages of life display something of a shift. Medieval representations often tended to be cyclical; with the Renaissance, we see the life course depicted in stepladder form. The career peaks at 40 or 50. These *Lebenstreppe* or *degrés des âges* created a model that would be used through the nineteenth century, and they could be viewed in part as a portrait of engagement in life's activities and in part as an image of pilgrimage or journey.

The journey might be seen as a secularized version of the pilgrimage, and the Renaissance held out the possibility of a more secular retreat. Minois sees a precursor to retirement in Jean le Bon's founding in 1351 of a home for old knights, what he calls "the first draft for the *Hôtel des Invalides* for elderly ex-servicemen" (Minois, p. 245). He refers to a hospital that received the elderly in Lyon and comparable institutions in Roubaix, London, Milan, and Paris, with beds reserved for old people in hospitals in smaller towns. And he uses the term "retirement" to describe the last years of a variety of notable individuals: Cosimo de Medici withdrawing in favor of his son Piero and writers Petrarch and Boccaccio retiring to country residences (p. 247).

In turning to literature, Minois sees "a cult of youth damning old age." He quotes from the sixteenth-century poetry of Ronsard. At 60:

> All that's left of me is bones. I resemble a skeleton,
> Unfleshed, unstrung, unmuscled and unpadded,
> Unmercifully struck down by the delineaments of death.
> I daren't view my arms for fear lest they tremble.
> *(p. 250)*

He draws upon poetry of France, England, Spain, and Italy, and he finds particularly ugly representations of aged women, quite reminiscent of the stereotypes of ancient comedy. In claiming two models for sixteenth-century life, he points to the courtier as delineated by Castiglione and the humanist as embodied by Erasmus. Both "rejected old people" (p. 258). The most recent scholarship paints a more nuanced position, but Minois' strong opinions give us something with which to debate:

> For Renaissance man, both the humanist and the courtier, old age remained the sign of the ultimate failure of their attempts to create superman. For old age makes us lose all the virtues of ideal man: beauty, strength, the capacity for decision and intellectual growth. It robs us of love and the worldly pleasures. It brings suffering and frailty. It was indeed that century's bugbear, which the utopians dreamt of abolishing.
> *(p. 287)*

Addressing the challenges of aging was not simply a utopian effort. The Renaissance and the subsequent early modern era saw an important literature, growing out of ancient and medieval medical and scientific texts, on the prolongation of life, resistance to the ailments of age, and the dream of a better existence. The most recent historian of prolongation of human life, David Boyd Haycock, sees a break with medieval tradition in the seventeenth-century writings of Francis Bacon and René Descartes. For Haycock, "Bacon's *History of Life and Death*, in the depth of its detail and the range of its applications and speculations, was a work unprecedented" (Haycock, p. 5). He goes on to trace modern ideas of perfectibility and progress in a scientific approach to the body, and he identifies Descartes at the beginning of a trend toward seeing the study of the brain and nervous system at the center of life and aging.

Science was offering a way to understand the aging process. The Book of Nature, in certain circles, would soon take precedence over the Book of Scripture. The strands of secular thought that came out of the Renaissance would lead to new forms of intellectual activity in the Scientific Revolution and the Enlightenment. Newly centralized states and increasingly wealthy cities would characterize early modern Europe. We turn next to aging in that era.

Works Cited and Further Reading

On East Asia, see Christie W. Kiefer, "Aging in Eastern Cultures: A Historical Overview," chapter 4 in *Handbook of the Humanities and Aging*, edited by Thomas R. Cole, David D. Van Tassel, and Robert Kastenbaum (NY: Springer, 1992); on the literature that seeks to relativize belief in "traditional respect" for the aged, see Susanne Formanek and Sepp Linhart, eds., *Aging: Asian Concepts and Experiences, Past and Present*, (Vienna: Verlag der Österreichischen Akademie der Wissenschaften, 1997); on Japan in particular, see Patrick Beillevaire, "Japan: a Household Society," in *A History of the Family*, Vol. 1, *Distant Worlds, Ancient Worlds*, edited by André Burguière, Christiane Klapisch-Zuber, Martine Segalen, and Françoise Zonabend (Cambridge: Harvard University Press, 1996).

Thomas R. Cole and Mary G. Winkler, eds., *The Oxford Book of Aging: Reflections on the Journey of Life* (NY: Oxford University Press, 1994) reprints a few Islamic texts, including excerpts from Rudaki, "Lament in Old Age," p. 312, and Rumi, *Masnavi*, p. 98. On early and medieval Islamic representations of aging, see Thomas J. O'Shaughnessy, "The Qur'anic View of Youth and Old Age," *Zeitschrift der Deutschen Morgenländischen Gesellschaft*, no. 141 (1991): 33–51, and Hasan Shuraydi, *The Raven and the Falcon: Youth versus Old Age in Medieval Arabic Literature* (Leiden: Brill, 2014). On the medieval Arab family, Thierry Bianquis, *La famille arabe médiévale* (Brussels: Editions complexe, 2005). On Islam and medicine, see Fazhur Rahman, *Health and Medicine in the Islamic Tradition* (NY: Crossroad, 1987); Harold G. Koenig and Saad Al Shohaib, *Health and Well-Being in Islamic Societies: Background, Research, and Applications* (NY: Springer, 2014). Said Nursi's treatise on old age: http://erisale.com/index.jsp?locale=en#content.en.203.286. For print version, see *The Flashes Collection* (Istanbul: Sözler Nesriyat A.S., 1995), translated by Şükran Vahide. Among the many recent works in English on Nursi, see, in particular, Ibrahim M. Abu-Rabi', ed. *Islam at the Crossroads: On the Life and Thought of Bediuzzaman Said Nursi* (Albany: SUNY Press, 2003); Ibrahim M. Abu-Rabi', ed., *Spiritual Dimensions of Bediuzzaman Said Nursi's* Risale-i Nur (Albany: SUNY Press, 2008); Serif Mardin, *Religion and Social Change in Modern Turkey: The Case of Bediüzzaman Said Nursi* (Albany: SUNY Press, 1989); Colin Turner, *The Qur'an Revealed: A Critical Analysis of Said Nursi's* Epistles of Light (Berlin: Gerlach Press, 2013), which includes a long treatment of the treatise on old age; Colin Turner and Hasan Horkuc, *Said Nursi* (London: I.B. Tauris, 2009), the most concise introduction; and Şükran Vahide, *Islam in Modern Turkey: An*

Intellectual Biography of Bediüzzaman Said Nursi (Albany: SUNY Press, 2005). For more recent Arabic literature, see Roger Allen, "Old Age in Arabic Literature," in Prisca von Dorotka and Patricia Spencer Soper, eds., *Perspectives on Aging in Literature: A Cross-cultural Study* (NY: Greenwood Press, 1989), pp. 113–130. For graffiti artist Islam Ahmad El Said's use of an aged character, see the film (DVD) *Graffiti Baladi* by Lisa Klemenz and Leslie Villiaume; it accompanies the book *Graffiti Baladi: Street Art et Révolution en Egypte*, text by Heba Farouk Mahfouz and Rana Al Hassanein (Montreuil: Omniscience, 2014).

On medieval representations of the ages of man, see John A. Burrow, *The Ages of Man: A Study in Medieval Writing and Thought* (Oxford: Oxford University Press, 1986), and Elizabeth Sears, *The Ages of Man: Medieval Interpretations of the Life Cycle* (Princeton: Princeton University Press, 1986). On the Middle Ages, see Shulamith Shahar, "Old Age in the High and Late Middle Ages: Image, Expectation and Status," in *Old Age from Antiquity to Post-Modernity*, edited by Paul Johnson and Pat Thane (London: Routledge, 1998), and her fuller survey of medieval aging, *Growing Old in the Middle Ages: "Winter Clothes us in Shadow and Pain"* (London: Routledge, 1997). For a look at the changing functions of families, with observations on intergenerational relations and property arrangements beginning in the Middle Ages, see Michael Mitterauer and Reinhard Sieder, *The European Family: Patriarchy to Partnership from the Middle Ages to the Present* (Chicago: University of Chicago Press, 1982). See also David G. Troyansky, "The Older Person in the Western World: From the Middle Ages to the Industrial Revolution," chapter 2 in *Handbook of the Humanities and Aging*. For a more focused examination of aging in one medieval society, see Joel Rosenthal, *Old Age in Late Medieval England* (Philadelphia: University of Pennsylvania Press, 1996). On religious retreat or "retirement," see Marie-Thérèse Lorcin, "Retraite des veuves et filles au couvent: Quelques aspects de la condition féminine à la fin du moyen âge," *Annales de Démographie Historique* (1975), pp. 187–204; Kirsi Salonen, "What Happened to Aged Priests in the Late Middle Ages?" in *On Old Age: Approaching Death in Antiquity and the Middle Ages*, edited by Christian Krötzl and Katariina Mustakallio (Turnhout: Brepols, 2011). On family and security, see Elaine Clark, "Some Aspects of Social Security in Medieval England," *Journal of Family History*, Vol. 7 (1982): pp. 307–320; on testamentary practices, see Samuel K. Cohn, Jr., *Death and Property in Siena, 1205–1800: Strategies for the Afterlife* (Baltimore: Johns Hopkins University Press, 1988). On youth and age, see Georges Duby, *A History of Private Life: 2. Revelations of the Medieval World* (Cambridge, MA: Harvard University Press, 1988). For families in one well-documented region, see David Herlihy and Christiane Klapisch-Zuber, *Tuscans and their Families: A Study of the Florentine Catasto of 1427* (New Haven: Yale University Press, 1985). For central Europe, see Katalin Szende, "Coping with Old Age in Medieval Hungarian Towns," in Krötzl and Mustakallio.

On medieval and early modern widowhood, see Sandra Cavallo and Lyndan Warner, eds., *Widowhood in Medieval and Early Modern Europe* (New York:

Longman, 1999); Emmanuelle Santinelli, *Des femmes éplorées?: les veuves dans la société aristocratique du haut Moyen âge* (Villeneuve-d'Ascq: Presses universitaires du Septentrion, 2003); Stephanie Fink De Backer, *Widowhood in Early Modern Spain: Protectors, Proprietors, and Patrons* (Leiden: Brill, 2010); Josette Brun, *Vie et mort du couple en Nouvelle-France: Québec et Louisbourg au XVIIIe siècle* (Montreal: McGill-Queens University Press, 2006); Scarlett Beauvalet-Boutouyrie, *Être veuve sous l'ancien régime* (Paris: Belin, 2001); and Janine Lanza, *From Wives to Widows in Early Modern Paris: Gender, Economy, and Law* (Aldershot: Ashgate, 2007).

On Renaissance aging, see the sources reprinted in Georges Minois, *History of Old Age: from Antiquity to the Renaissance* (Chicago: University of Chicago Press, 1989). For more nuanced views, see Colette H. Winn and Cathy Yandell, eds., *Vieillir à la Renaissance* (Paris: Honoré Champion, 2009); Erin Campbell, ed., *Growing Old in Early Modern Europe* (Farnham and Burlington: Ashgate, 2006).

On Shakespeare and aging, see Anthony Ellis, *Old Age, Masculinity, and Early Modern Drama: Comic Elders on the Italian and Shakespearean Stage* (Farnham and Burlington, Ashgate, 2009); Maurice Charney, *Wrinkled Deep in Time: Aging in Shakespeare* (NY: Columbia UP, 2009). For aging in art, see Christine Dayonnet and Jean Lasserre, *La vieillesse dans l'art occidental* (Toulouse: Université du Troisième Âge, 1982); Caroline Schuster Cardone, *Le crépuscule du corps: images de la vieillesse féminine* (Gollion, Switzerland: Infolio, 2009). For early modern and modern prolongevity, see David Boyd Haycock, *Mortal Coil: A Short History of Living Longer* (New Haven: Yale University Press, 2009).

5

EARLY MODERN AGING AND THE AGED IN EUROPE AND NORTH AMERICA

The period that follows the Renaissance in Europe is characterized by some very big changes. The humanistic themes of Renaissance culture would outlive the period and develop in important ways, stimulated in part by the invention of the printing press. Texts that had previously been communicated in manuscript, if at all, now appeared in print form, and educated persons had easier access to classical thought. That thought included ancient texts on aging, from philosophical treatments to medical opinion. The early modern period would then see considerable discussion of ways of countering the challenges of advancing age.

At the same time, Europe underwent fundamental restructuring in religious, economic, and political terms. The Reformations recast the relationship between the secular and the sacred and had an important impact on the idea of the individual. The emergence of capitalism remade everyday life, and the emergence of global markets drew diverse peoples into new relations. The growth of nation states remade the political world and provided new structures of power. The cultural and political changes that quickened in the eighteenth century, resulting in the Enlightenment and the French Revolution, represented an important step towards modernity.

All these developments had repercussions for the elderly. For example, the Protestant Reformation encouraged individualism and personal reflection and writing; the results included a strengthened patriarchy but also widespread reflection upon the experience of growing old. The Catholic Reformation strengthened traditional religious institutions, but it cast serious attention upon the spiritual self, including thought about aging and preparation for death, and encouraged the founding of hospitals and hospices that catered, among others, to the aged.

Cutting across the different confessions, the Reformations of the sixteenth and seventeenth centuries represented a shift in consciousness about spiritual issues, and among them were those associated with the confrontation with aging and death. Historians see the Reformations as contributing to the disciplining of Europe in particular ways. They had an impact on the meaning of family life and of death. Historians often emphasize a strengthening of patriarchy as supported by religious thinking, but some point to the emergence of greater companionship between spouses and between parents and children. Protestant imagery included depiction of the patriarch reading the Bible to his household; in many versions, it is an elder. Protestant Europe saw a proliferation of images of family life. Catholic imagery included aged saints, and Catholic preaching revived earlier Christian calls for contempt for the world and mortification of the body. As one popular religious text, railing against the vanity of earthly existence, put it: "the actions of old people are cowardly, negligent, slothful, frigid, coarse, defective, trembling, accompanied by sorrow and *ennui*" (Troyansky, p. 85). Protestant preaching in Europe and colonial North America could also warn against vanity, seeing that sin as especially common in advanced age.

Religious devotion in the period of the Reformations encouraged self-consciousness. Journal-writing comes down to us and reveals a sense of dealing with the passage of time, of the richness of personal experience and the succession of losses that come with disease and death. We have reports on grandparenthood, long friendship, and hopes for salvation. Individual accounts of growing old appear in a variety of histories of old age, but probably the best studied first-person writing on old age in the early modern period is found in England beginning in the seventeenth and eighteenth centuries. In part it was a result of religious concerns of dissenting Protestants—aging individuals in those groups were quite concerned with their souls—but a range of individuals left life-histories. Lynn Botelho and Susannah Ottaway have made an important selection in a multi-volume documentary history of old age, and selection was necessary. More than 332 English diaries survive from the seventeenth century, and more than 735 diaries from the eighteenth century are known. Many were kept into late life. So they serve as sources, but their very existence makes a point. Some are daily accounts and others are more retrospective memoirs, allowing us a glimpse into what people remembered over the course of their lives (*The History of Old Age in England, 1600–1800*).

One English diary, studied in great detail by Anne Kugler, concerns the life of Sarah, Lady Cowper, from her 50s to her 70s in the very early eighteenth century. Kugler points out that Lady Cowper expressed a "religious understanding of the world alongside her increasing skepticism of the supernatural," and she identifies the author's reading as including works of piety, popular medicine, and social comportment. Through that reading and her own familial and social experience, she came up with a way of approaching old age (Botelho and Ottaway, vol. 7, p. vii).

First-person writing reveals those who are secure in their faith and standing and those who express fear. Intense fears might involve thoughts of the afterlife, but they might also focus on the everyday supernatural. Witch-hunting had been particularly common in some parts of Europe in the sixteenth and seventeenth centuries, and while those accused of being witches were not necessarily elderly, they were certainly older than their medieval counterparts, and the association of age with witchcraft would survive in popular culture and even modern mass culture. The object of fear, the aged "witch" could also be seen as a person with significant power. Some historians see gerontophobia as one result; others see psychological insecurity. But by the late seventeenth century, witch-hunting was very much on the decline, a function of suppression by both church and state.

Recent scholarship indicates a kinder view of the aged in a universe of Protestant piety and institutions, although there is evidence that the Reformation in England temporarily harmed the aged poor because of declines in charitable support. Puritan New England is a place that has been depicted as favorable to the aged, and the Dutch Republic portrayed sympathetic images of family life and of kind old teachers. While some religious individuals might have faced their last days with fear and trembling, some Protestants saw survival to a good old age itself as a sign of election. Calvinist churches were structured to permit the authority of elders, and depictions of guild life in the Netherlands suggest an association between age and authority. Associational life encouraged the creation of some old age homes, with Protestant and Jewish examples in the Netherlands, and Catholic institutions in Italy and France included hospitals specializing in care of the aged.

Hospitals were repositories not only of the sick and aged but of the unwanted more generally. Municipalities and states founded some such institutions. Religious orders did the same. They began earliest in northern and central Europe, emerging later on in Italy and France. While it's not at all clear that hospitals managed to separate themselves dramatically from medieval medical practices or even to do much more than house the undifferentiated poor and abandoned, they did begin a long-term process of specialization, and some became identified with the aged. In Paris, La Salpêtrière, which would play an even more important scientific role in the nineteenth and twentieth centuries, had a large population of women over 60 but also the poor, the blind, and the insane (not that these are mutually exclusive categories); Bicêtre housed aged men but also served generally as a place of confinement. Old soldiers were housed in the Hôtel Royal des Invalides, and the neighborhood surrounding it catered to an aging clientele.

Philosophical texts by Francis Bacon and René Descartes set not only a philosophical agenda for modernity but also a scientific and medical one concerning life extension. Scientific texts proliferated and medical practices and dietary regimes designed to extend life became increasingly common. The aged body would be dissected, and occupational hazards identified. Scientific discourse retained some aspects of classical thought but displayed a new interest in empirical observation. Newly generated data on rates of mortality and life expectancy put discussion of the life course on a more scientific footing. Quantitative understanding of life derived less and less from classical traditions of the ages of life and more from study by physicians, mathematicians, and political authorities. Those authorities ranged from municipalities to the increasingly powerful nation states, and thus emerged political economy, which measured the strength of populations. States also began organizing pension schemes for particular groups of civil servants. They rooted them in the mathematics of probability and life expectancy. Looking back at the early modern era, we see contemporary efforts to understand the ages of life.

The state made for significant change and the development of European hegemony over the world. Beyond the expression of power, the state meant order and administration, especially in the period that followed the religious warfare that dominated the sixteenth century and the first half of the seventeenth. And the increasing presence of the state infiltrated people's lives. Slowly, states developed systems of pensions for their servants and rules for thinking about careers and their ends. The Customs Service in England and the Tax Farmers in France were among the earliest to receive pensions associated with careers. States offered pensions to some active individuals who remained in service or were deemed worthy of reward; they experimented with recompensing those who had completed long-term service. The nineteenth century would see further developments in this area that had important early modern precursors.

The emergence of a world market in the early modern period resulted in new activities that in some cases were less reliant upon physical labor but in others involved the intensification of production. At times this meant the possibility of remaining active even as the body grew weaker; at other times it meant greater difficulty as one aged. One cannot generalize; it is necessary to look very closely at local contexts, and historians of old age have been doing just that, particularly in England, France, and colonial North America. It is possible that older people in the early modern period faced some of the same challenges as their modern and contemporary counterparts in terms of whether it was advantageous to reside in city or country. In rural areas that lost population to nearby cities, older people could be left behind by younger emigrants, and so locally populations might be unusually aged. But that's something we discover retrospectively. For inhabitants of seventeenth-century England, for example, it would not have made much sense to speak of an aged population. The aged were recognized by physical signs of decline, but they still tried to maintain autonomy. Nonetheless, there was some sense of obligation on the part of kin and community to look after the dependent elderly.

Lynn Botelho has studied the aged in the context of the English Poor Laws, which had emerged in the sixteenth century and been codified in the early seventeenth, and she confirms the existence of community obligation toward the weak and elderly. She also shows how the context changed with the emergence of capitalism. Poor Law Overseers turned their attention from the elderly and weak towards poor people who were capable of laboring in workhouses. According to Botelho, in the shift to a cash and credit economy in the last decades of the seventeenth century, the elderly lost out, and she finds a cultural shift. "Rather than the elderly being revered primarily for their wisdom and spiritual maturity, respect was also now to be gained by their self-sufficiency and ability to live without the help of the government, their families or their neighbours" (Botelho and Ottaway, vol. 5, p. xi). In a world of money, individuals were to accrue savings and be responsible for themselves. For the large number who could not save, the results were unfortunate. And when families had to choose between helping elders or children, they seem to have looked to the future. Pat Thane warns us against assuming much coresidence between adult generations. She points out that a third of women living to 65 in the sixteenth and seventeenth centuries had no surviving child. That would change somewhat, but still in the late eighteenth century one fifth were in that position. Steven Ruggles argues that it was the nineteenth century, with high rates of migration, that saw more extended families.

Historians have debated the efficacy of the Old Poor Law. Susannah Ottaway points out that while some have seen it as "restrictive and parsimonious," others see it as something that the aged might "count on" (Ottaway, p. 9). Thomas Sokoll, examining the late eighteenth and early nineteenth centuries, claims that "while support for the elderly could be fairly generous under the Old Poor Law, this was by no means the norm" (Thane, p. 159). Ottaway's analysis of its operation in the eighteenth century contends that "parishes…gave such substantial pensions to such a significant proportion of the elderly in their communities, that it seems logical to conclude that any aging person living in these parishes would have felt that they were extremely likely to qualify for a pension should they fall into absolute impotence and poverty in their old age" (Ottaway, p. 10). She finds more and more people in need of such support as the cost of living was going up. Thus, she contends that the poor elderly would be increasingly seen as burdens on the parish and, hence, as constituting a "clearly definable subset of the population." In that sense, they pointed to the nineteenth-century idea of the pensioner and to the modern notion of old age as coming at a particular age. But already in the eighteenth century, she finds increasing recourse to pensions and the development of friendly societies aimed at mutual aid in time of emergency or disability. To some extent, mutual aid grew out of a sense of social solidarity, but it also needs to be understood as being rooted in a world of individual effort, savings, and responsibility. At the same time, the workhouse was becoming more important. It symbolized a more industrious economy and society. It also responded to socio-economic differences and, thus, different forms of aging. The institutionalized old person would play a different role from the elder at home.

At a time when new forms of economic activities included capitalist risk-taking and investment, urban people with money to spend invested in private pensions and *tontines*. Middle-class people could purchase *rentes* from other individuals and institutions, which made regular payments in return. *Tontines* took in payments from all members and generated wealth for investors who survived longer than their fellows. Such a system was a primitive form of insurance.

Betting on one's survival was a haphazard thing, but people in northwestern Europe were surviving longer. Life expectancy went up in the eighteenth century, but we should not confuse that with population aging. Indeed, increased fertility in England translated into a "younger" population. That didn't stop adults from living longer. It is not the dramatic demographic shift that would begin in Europe in the mid-nineteenth century, but it certainly represented a change when compared to the seventeenth. A 25-year-old could expect to live another 30.4 years in the period 1640–1689, another 35.4 years in the period 1750–1809 (Botelho and Ottaway, vol. 6, p. x). Scholars of France have also demonstrated increased life expectancy and an awareness of the challenges of growing old. We will look more closely at the cultural shift associated with that awareness in the next chapter.

The "long eighteenth century" (from late seventeenth to early nineteenth) can be seen as the end of an early modern period characterized by continuity and as the coming of modernity, a period of intellectual change and political revolt. It also saw significant demographic and economic growth, the beginnings of the growth associated with industrialization and what has sometimes been called a commercial revolution. Why Europe and the Atlantic world rather than China became the center of an emerging world economy has been a subject of great historical debate, but that domination by Europe shaped international relations into the twentieth century.

The Enlightenment is the name given to the intellectual and cultural movement of the eighteenth century that saw a shift from a religious worldview to a secular one. This meant the application of scientific ideas to a variety of pursuits, including what would be seen eventually as the social sciences. The connection to aging was twofold. First the secularization (described by some historians as dechristianization) evident in the period meant a greater focus on this world rather than the next. For old people this meant the replacement of an otherworldly afterlife by earthly posterity, and for some aging women writers it meant an exploration of alternative ways of searching for dignity, a time for love and not just pious preparation for death. Second, the emergence of the social sciences included broader interest in population, economy, and society. Early demographic study, with roots in England in the seventeenth century, became relatively common in the North American colonies, and ideas about insurance took hold in the Anglo-American world around the time of the American Revolution. Ways of thinking that would eventually become second nature were newly invented.

The end of the eighteenth century saw political revolutions on both sides of the Atlantic Ocean. The language of these revolutions derived from Enlightenment thought; the events transformed public order and people's senses of self and history; the institutions they created hinted at concerns for the elderly. The American Revolution could be seen as yielding the enshrinement of revolutionaries as founding fathers whose legacy continued to play an active political and cultural role; the French Revolution involved the overthrow of an Old Regime, but it also held out the possibility of creating a society free from old age poverty and of honoring its elderly in newly invented public festivals. The Revolutionary era also offers a bridge to the nineteenth century.

Works Cited and Further Reading

David G. Troyansky, *Old Age in the Old Regime: Image and Experience in Eighteenth-Century France* (Ithaca: Cornell University Press, 1989); Lynn Botelho and Susannah Ottaway, eds., *The History of Old Age in England, 1600–1800*, 8 volumes (London: Pickering and Chatto, 2008–2009). Parts of the Lady Cowper diary appear in *The History of Old Age in England*; but for an analysis of the diary in the context of first-person writing and the history of the family, gender, and aging, see Anne Kugler, *Errant Plagiary: The Life and Writing of Lady Sarah Cowper, 1644–1720* (Stanford: Stanford University Press, 2002).

On witchcraft and age, see Edward Bever, "Old Age and Witchcraft in Early Modern Europe," in Peter N. Stearns, ed., *Old Age in Preindustrial Society* (NY: Holmes and Meier, 1982), pp. 150–190. More generally on witchcraft, see Brian P. Levack, *The Witch-Hunt in Early Modern Europe* (New York and London: Longman, 1995); Lyndal Roper, *Oedipus and the Devil: Witchcraft, Sexuality and Religion in Early Modern Europe* (London: Routledge, 1994).

For some immediate consequences of the Reformation in England, see Claire Schen, "Strategies of Poor Aged Women and Widows in Sixteenth-century London," in Lynn Botelho and Pat Thane, eds., *Women and Ageing in British Society Since 1500* (Harlow: Pearson, 2001), pp. 13–30. For old age in colonial New England, see the relevant chapter in John Demos, *Past, Present, and Personal: The Family and the Life Course in American History* (NY: Oxford University Press, 1986). For a historian's use of Dutch paintings and prescriptive literature, see Simon Schama, *The Embarrassment of Riches: An Interpretation of Dutch Culture in the Golden Age* (NY: Knopf, 1987). On old soldiers at the Invalides, see Jean-Pierre Bois, *Les anciens soldats dans la société française au XVIIIe siècle* (Paris: Economica, 1990). For early modern approaches to old age, see the early chapters in Jean-Pierre Bois, *Les vieux: de Montaigne aux premières retraites* (Paris: Fayard, 1989). On early pensions (and much else), see Josef Ehmer, *Sozialgeschichte des Alters* (Frankfurt: Suhrkamp, 1990). On probability and life expectancy, see Jacques Dupâquier and Michel Dupâquier, *Histoire de la démographie* (Paris: Perrin, 1985); Lorraine Daston, *Classical Probability in the Enlightenment* (Princeton: Princeton University Press, 1988). On British pensions, see Marios Raphael, *Pensions and Public Servants: A Study of the Origins of the British System* (Paris: Mouton, 1964); for European comparisons, see Bois, *Les vieux*, pp. 228–231, 387–392. Pat Thane, *Old Age in English History: Past Experiences, Present Issues* (Oxford: Oxford University Press, 2000). Steven Ruggles, *Prolonged Connections: the Rise of the Extended Family in England and America* (Madison: University of Wisconsin Press, 1987).

Susannah Ottaway, *The Decline of Life: Old Age in Eighteenth-Century England* (Cambridge: Cambridge University Press, 2004). On secularization or dechristianization, see Michel Vovelle, *Piété baroque et déchristianisation: Les attitudes devant la mort en Provence au XVIIIe siècle* (Paris: Plon, 1973); John McManners, *Death and the Enlightenment: Changing Attitudes to Death among Christians and Unbelievers in*

Eighteenth-Century France (Oxford: Oxford University Press, 1981). On gender and aging in the eighteenth century, see Joan Hinde Stewart, *The Enlightenment of Age: Women, Letters, and Growing Old in Eighteenth-Century France* (Oxford: Voltaire Foundation, 2010). For the emergence of the social sciences, see Keith Michael Baker, *Condorcet: From Natural Philosophy to Social Mathematics* (Chicago: University of Chicago Press, 1975); for early demography, see James H. Cassedy, *Demography in Early America: Beginnings of the Statistical Mind, 1600–1800* (Cambridge: Harvard University Press, 1969). Peter C. Hoffer, *Revolution and Regeneration, Life Cycle and the Historical Vision of the Generation of 1776* (Athens: University of Georgia Press, 1983).

SECTION III
Transitions to Modernity

6

CULTURAL TRANSITIONS AND IMPLICATIONS FOR THE AGED

The eighteenth and nineteenth centuries saw the emergence of the aged individual in various guises. French historians have made the strongest case for a major cultural shift associated with the Enlightenment beginning in the middle of the eighteenth century. David Troyansky identified a change from a religious approach to old age and a focus on the next world (Augustinian retreat) to a more secular approach to late life and the possibility of still playing an earthly role (Ciceronian retirement). He piled up examples from religious texts, books of devotion, and sermons to philosophical, scientific, and medical treatises, and graphic and literary representations. Cicero's *De Senectute* was often reprinted and translated, and authors began to write about women's aging as well, with Madame de Lambert consciously imitating Cicero. Joan Hinde Stewart's close reading of a few French women writers indicates how some individuals, particularly in personal letters, challenged cultural constraints. Works of theater and fiction paid increasing attention to old age, and traditional comical representations of the elderly gave way to more respectful and sentimental depictions.

Jean-Pierre Gutton and Jean-Pierre Bois confirmed the shift. Bois showed how old age was "no longer a rare chance for a few, but the natural completion of life" (Bois, p. 152). Practitioners of "political arithmetic" deployed data on the ages of life and began depicting populations in the form of age pyramids. Bois even wrote that "old age was born in 1760" (p. 158). Not that there was something magical about that one year, but the attention that old age drew in cultural production at that moment is striking. And while he also concentrated on French sources, speaking of the "French invention of the good old man," he demonstrated that all over Europe adults had a greater chance of living past 60, and he could point to parallel cultural developments in European literary and artistic expressions of sensibility and respect. In Italy the playwright Carlo Goldoni's old characters evolved from avaricious and misanthropic beings to prudent and virtuous ones. The wise old man who benefited from a lifetime's experience was becoming more visible, as was the loving grandmother. Bois sees a parallel with the development of the "noble savage," the good natural man, and finds the writer Denis Diderot, who made that theme his own, elaborating upon the roles of grandparents. He and Gutton both signal a simultaneous development in the "discovery" of both childhood and old age. A focus on children was more evident as was the value of "recognition, tenderness, and respect due the old man" (p. 196). Previously, the old woman might have been taken for a witch; now she was a grandmother, telling stories of witches to loving grandchildren. As we will see shortly, the relationship between grandparents and grandchildren would evolve in important ways in the nineteenth and twentieth centuries.

Historical investigation into the late eighteenth century has identified multiple developments related to the aged. Bois speaks of a "golden age of patriarchs" from 1760 to 1790 (p. 196), but he also describes the more needy aged. At home they would move among what he calls the "three stations" of old people: the bed, the table, and the bench. Patriarchal authority may have declined in one setting and been maintained in another. Either way, increased life expectancy meant visibility of the aged. They were not the idealized or ridiculed elderly of philosophy and literature, but simply old people present in everyday life.

One consequence of increasing life expectancy was a more common experience of coexistence of aged parents and adult children. Family structures varied across Europe and even within regions, but while coresidence of aged parents and adult children only existed in some places, in many others we know of generations that lived in fairly close proximity. Coresidence was not the only way to remain close. Nuclear households were most common in northwestern Europe, and more extended families were found to the east and south, but even in the northwest, in England and northern France, for example, independence did not necessarily mean isolation.

Historians have studied the kinds of arrangements made between generations, whether in marriage contracts, donations, or testaments. People who owned and worked the land drew up contracts calling for guaranteed support of aged parents. They had the documents notarized and referred to them when disputes arose. We cannot assume that people simply looked after each other; nor can we assume that the existence of maintenance contracts signified a complete lack of trust between family members. Maintenance contracts offered protection, an outline of what had to happen in case of dispute. They might call for a particular amount of food and drink to be provided, an itinerary by which aged parents moved from one child's home to another's, reservation of a bench, a bed, a room, or perhaps poignantly the right to walk in the fields and pick fruit. Just as the culture was calling for greater dignity for the aged, such contracts tried to offer minimal support and dignity in times of potential stress. One recent publication refers to such contracts as "pacts of governance" that helped avoid abusive conditions (Rameau, pp. 108–109).

The eighteenth century also saw the spread of institutions to help the aged. *Dépôts de mendicité*, which housed beggars in France, contained a range of ages that might include anywhere from 9% to 37% people over 60. In the Netherlands, poorhouses and hospitals proliferated, as they did in the German towns of Hanover, Berlin, Bremen, Göttingen, Augsburg, Karlsruhe, Weimar, Mainz, and Magdeburg. The Invalides served French veterans, and in 1790 1107 of the 3000 people housed and fed were between the ages of 70 and 92 (Bois, p. 227). The Invalides may have been most famous, but old soldiers were cared for in England, Austria, Prussia, and elsewhere. Sometimes old soldiers received assistance at home, and civil servants who had moved around during their careers increasingly enjoyed sedentary repose.

Awareness of the challenge of growing older and the possibility of intergenerational strife gave rise to greater thought about the needs of the elderly in the era of the French Revolution. Government ministries throughout Europe were moving steadily toward rewarding their employees, and revolutionary committees investigated the needs of the elderly as well as others who were in potentially weak positions. Philanthropy and humanitarianism were themes of the Enlightenment, and practical ideas for dealing with old age poverty made their way into Revolutionary-era public debates. Government reports were made on poverty and beggary, and pension plans were sketched out for a remarkable variety of citizens. Indeed, citizenship itself was a new phenomenon, and associated ideas of natural rights and human rights found their way into constitution writing and legislation. In the early phase of the French Revolution, a 1790 report on the need for pensions singled out people who made contributions to the sciences, letters, and arts as well as the military and civil functions. In the Revolutionary republic a 1793 committee that explored poverty and the need for social assistance sketched out ideas that look remarkably modern. They spoke of a right to assistance and a dignified old age. Thus, Revolutionary notions of human rights, mostly associated with political and civil rights, extended partly and theoretically to social and economic rights, anticipating those that would be achieved in the late nineteenth and twentieth centuries. In immediate practical terms, little was accomplished of a lasting nature. But a long public and international debate was beginning. The Revolutionary regime had pressing concerns about international and civil war, but it also sponsored a 1794 contest for the ideal peasant household, in which a banner would be draped, saying "Honorable repose after work." When young troops marched off to defend the Republic, they were to be urged on by elders.

A rhetoric of the life course was deployed in the Revolutionary system of secular festivals. Some Revolutionary festivals marked anniversaries of political events. They replaced religious festivals of the past. Others marked secular principles and stages of the life course: youth, marriage, old age. For the festival of old age, young people paid homage to their elders, who were paraded through the streets or village square and honored with speeches and theatrical performances. The French Revolution had tried to put an end to social divisions; it eliminated corporate bodies, replacing them with a world of individuals. In effect, biological divisions replaced social ones. Since all who lived out a "normal" life course could expect to experience the ages of life, these were distinctions that coexisted with a spirit of equality. Such expectation of long life was not yet as assured as it would come to be in the twentieth century, but it was already on the increase.

The individualism that grew out of the Enlightenment and the Atlantic Revolutions had an impact on aging, as the older person became a focus of attention by others, a character in culture that transcended traditional stereotypes, and the mature self in an increasingly secularized world. In the nineteenth century, an era that saw the development of political and cultural movements associated with youth, the old person remained visible and subject to sentimental representation. Following the American Revolution, the early republic began to look back at founding fathers. After a period in the early nineteenth century that saw youth as central to Romanticism in culture and politics, European states and societies in the second half of the century looked to notable elderly men and some women as key figures, and the role of grandparents took on new importance in European society.

Bois presents the early nineteenth century as an era that was hostile to old age. Inspired by Revolutionary movements of the turn of the century, European youth rallied to progressive and national causes. Young Italy and Young Germany were among several movements that expressed political Romanticism in their respective countries. In their political imaginations, youth represented republicanism and democracy while age seemed to embody absolutism and conservatism. Poets and artists associated with Romanticism turned to themes of youthful heroism and premature death, and consequently old age seemed absent for a time.

By the middle of the nineteenth century, and especially after the Revolutions of 1848, European culture turned again to aged subjects, and they did so both in realistic and sentimental veins, depending upon artist and author. Novels described the social experience of urban and rural people, among them the elderly. Portraiture and genre painting offered reflections of reality that ranged from the ideal to the sentimental to the naturalistic. Some of those writers and artists themselves embodied somewhat idealized national visions of the elderly. As Bois has put it, "To each nation, its old man: Hugo, Verdi, Tolstoy, Tennyson" (*Les vieux*, p. 392) As creators of aged characters who also continued to produce work of extraordinary quality into advanced age, they incarnated national memory both at home and abroad. And in 1877 Hugo published his poetry collection, *The Art of Being a Grandfather*.

The most important history of grandparenthood follows the existing literature on eighteenth-century developments, but Vincent Gourdon has discovered the "triumph" of the image of the grandparent who spoiled his or her grandchildren. In a process that extended from the middle of the eighteenth century into the nineteenth, the idea of the grandparent evolved from a reminder of lineage and ancestry to an emphasis on specific individuals and their affective relationships with their grandchildren. Books about grandparents and grandchildren proliferated in the second half of the nineteenth century (Gourdon, p. 74), but representations of grandparents varied by social and religious groups. Thus, old-fashioned ideas of grandparents as representing ancestry remained important in conservative, aristocratic, and Catholic circles while the image of the loving grandparent took hold in the middle class.

The new grandparent could indulge and spoil grandchildren, thus softening the authority of parents and mediating the often conflictual relationship between parents and children. Indulgent grandparents would not have had the real authority of early modern elders, but in the nineteenth century they had a new role to play in supplementing children's socialization. Visits to grandparents and vacations spent with them were important events in the raising of middle-class children. Formal education was in the hands of parents and schools, but grandparents could transmit values and ideals. Older women advised their own daughters as they became mothers and, especially if they retained their health, developed a special bond with their grandchildren. Gourdon sees the emergence of the spoiling grandparent as part of the coming to cultural power of the European middle classes. Memoir-writing in the nineteenth century often made important mention of grandparents and visits to their homes. Family rituals developed around holidays and, increasingly in the nineteenth and twentieth centuries, birthdays.

We know less about working-class and peasant grandparents than their middle-class counterparts—life expectancy varied by social class, of course—but there is evidence of the role of grandparents in storytelling, an important form of popular cultural transmission. And in rural villages that sent large numbers of young adults to work in cities, elders, including grandparents, had to have played a significant role. We will look again at their role in the contemporary world, but, as Gourdon puts it, the evolution of the grandparent from authority figure to loving confidant and even partner is the product not of the last few decades but of a two-hundred-year process that was not always directly linked to big demographic change.

The argument that cultural change concerning old age was independent of big demographic changes is at the heart of W. Andrew Achenbaum's history of old age in the United States. As he writes,

> Continuities and changes in the way Americans thought about elderly men and women before 1914 did not simply reflect shifts in the relative number of people over sixty in society, variations in the proportion of older workers in the labor force, or alterations in the perception and treatment of the aged poor. Ideas about the worth and functions of the elderly have a life of their own.
> *(Achenbaum, p. 86)*

What he found in nineteenth-century America was different from what Bois and Gourdon found for France and Europe more generally. For him the idea that mattered most was that of the obsolescence of old age.

Thomas Cole's cultural history of aging in America sees more than denigration in the nineteenth century, but he seems to agree that in that period "old age lost its ideological prestige" (Cole, p. 56). Still, he provides a rich description of competing cultural representations. He claims that a "late Calvinist ideal of aging" survived in some quarters well into the nineteenth century, but he sees a change. "Taken broadly, advice about aging in the nineteenth century underwent a shift from consolation and mystery to exhortation and mastery – what a later era might label from pessimism to optimism" (p. 67). It's not some simple shift from religious to secular attitudes, but even representations of aging that included religious ideas were evolving.

> Once expectation of long life achieved widespread cultural sanction in the mid-nineteenth century (and this preceded the actual demographic accomplishment of increased longevity), gratitude and humility came to appear less appropriate. The sense of being fortunate gave way to the desire to remove the misfortunes and infirmities of age.
>
> *(p. 68)*

For older men in particular, what had been a masculine image associated with patriarchy gave way to "more emotional characteristics increasingly associated with feminine virtue" (p. 69).

A sentimental and sometimes secular image then emerged, as writings on both sides of the Atlantic presented readers with a new old man. "Coleridge's Ancient Mariner, Wordsworth's Old Cumberland Beggar, and Washington Irving's Rip Van Winkle all convey a strangeness mixed with the poignancy of nostalgia" (p. 74). Religious writings still appealed to American readers seeking consolation, but Victorian-era writings on old age included both evangelical and secular calls for self-reliance and health. Cole describes a "middle-class quest for a normal life course" (p. 111). The Calvinist emphasis on "putting off the old man," a reference to the aging body, and preparation for death, was giving way to an ideal of preparing for long life. As Longfellow put it in his *Morituri Salutamus*:

> For age is opportunity no less
> Than youth itself, though in another dress,
> And as the evening twilight fades away
> The sky is filled with stars, invisible by day.
> *(p. 155)*

By the last decades of the nineteenth century, Cole argues, the Victorian vision of a good old age was in decline. In a world of capitalist enterprise and the growing importance of science, things turned in a direction comparable to the obsolescence evoked by Achenbaum, and Cole describes what he calls the new "scientific management of aging" in the late nineteenth and early twentieth centuries. In that same era, it became increasingly common for people to be aware of their own and others' ages (Chudacoff).

Science and medicine played an increasing role in the study of old age, as so much of life would become medicalized. Although one can point to an important contribution to the study of the aging body back in the early American republic with the work of Benjamin Rush, the center for the medical study of aging was Paris, where research hospitals played an influential role. Although German medicine rose to preeminence late in the nineteenth century, the works on the aged produced in France continued to have influence into the twentieth century, when the center of research moved across the Atlantic to the United States. What tied them together was a dual mission, to study physical and psychological manifestations of aging and to discover ways of treating the ailments of the aged.

The transformation of old age in the eighteenth and nineteenth centuries involved shifts in religious and secular views, images of the aged in middle-class families, specialization of hospitals for the elderly, and the increasingly important role of grandparents. We must also pay attention to the image and experience of the pensioner. But before we do that, we will examine demographic transitions.

Works Cited and Further Reading

David G. Troyansky, *Old Age in the Old Regime: Image and Experience in Eighteenth-Century France* (Ithaca: Cornell University Press, 1989); Joan Hinde Stewart, *The Enlightenment of Age: Women, Letters, and Growing Old in Eighteenth-Century France* (Oxford: Voltaire Foundation, 2010); Jean-Pierre Gutton, *Naissance du vieillard: essai sur l'histoire des rapports entre les vieillards et la société en France* (Paris: Aubier, 1988); Jean-Pierre Bois, *Les vieux: de Montaigne aux premières retraites* (Paris: Fayard, 1989). On contracts between generations, see Angélique Rameau, "Garantir et vivre ses vieux jours en milieu rural (Xe–Xxe siècles): Eléments de réflexion sur les stratégies des acteurs ruraux pour organiser les conditions de leur vieillesse," in Laetitia Guerlain and Hinda Hedhili, eds., *Vieillir à travers les âges: Retraites et dépendance* (Paris, 2012). On age and Revolutionary festivals, see Mona Ozouf, *Festivals and the French Revolution* (Cambridge, MA: Harvard University Press, 1988). On grandparents, see Vincent Gourdon, *Histoire des grands-parents* (Paris: Perrin, 2001).

Among American histories, see W. Andrew Achenbaum, *Old Age in the New Land: The American Experience since 1790* (Baltimore: The Johns Hopkins University Press, 1978); Thomas Cole, *The Journey of Life: A Cultural History of Aging in America* (NY: Cambridge University Press, 1992); Howard Chudacoff, *How Old Are You? Age Consciousness in American Culture* (Princeton: Princeton University Press, 1989).

# 7

DEMOGRAPHIC TRANSITIONS AND IMPLICATIONS FOR THE AGED

As we saw in the previous chapter, cultural shifts surrounding old age beginning in the second half of the eighteenth century occurred against the backdrop of some lengthening of the average life span for individuals in the Western world. It was not dramatic, and it was not yet the beginning of the population aging that would occur from the middle of the nineteenth century into the twentieth and twenty-first. But it did mean a greater visibility of the aged and children's greater familiarity with grandparents. At the same time, Enlightenment-era literature focused new attention on population and social welfare, and French Revolutionary legislators and administrators identified emerging needs of vulnerable populations as well as the rhetorical uses of old persons in stabilizing regimes. The era of the French Revolution also marked an inflection point in the demographic history of Europe, with important implications worldwide.

One of the ways in which historians have defined modernity has been through population trends characteristic of the last couple of centuries. Historical demographers speak of an old demographic regime and a new one. The old regime was characterized by high death rates and high birth rates, in a kind of balance described as it was coming to an end at the turn of the nineteenth century by Thomas Malthus (*An Essay on the Principle of Population*). The new regime involved reduced death rates and birth rates. As we will see, the transition from one to the other could occur as rapidly as a few decades in the less developed world of the second half of the twentieth century and as long as a couple of centuries (or more) among some Western Europeans beginning around 1800. How world populations have transformed themselves has varied from place to place. Scholarship undertaken from the 1960s through the 1980s attempted to draw a vast portrait of fertility decline across Europe, but the evidence failed to confirm one model followed everywhere. Nonetheless, the basic ingredients have been loosely comparable. Demographers focus principally on rates of birth, marriage, and death; they also examine rates of migration. Migration in the modern world has usually involved movement from country to city and along international paths, and marital rates have varied significantly from place to place, but the key variables in what has been called the demographic transition have been births and deaths.

Over the long term, birth rates and death rates have both come down, as methods of contraception have become more effective and public health measures, education, nutrition, and medicine have had their impacts. The international history of the demographic transition is characterized by differences in timing. In some places, birth rates declined first and death rates followed. But more often, mortality decline preceded fertility decline, and the natural result was population growth. More reliable sources of food, cleaner water, the disappearance of plague, and small but consequential climatic change (a warmer eighteenth century after the "Little Ice Age" of the seventeenth) made a difference on the mortality side. Equilibrium was eventually achieved, as populations learned to bring down birthrates. But virtually everywhere, the two big trends were among the fundamental facts of modern historical experience, and historians have explored the connection between those trends and economic changes associated with urbanization and industrialization. In some places, industrial development permitted households to form early, and rates of marriage went up. Population growth from early marriage and falling death rates also had an impact on the economy, as more people meant both more producers and more consumers.

In those places where death rates came down first but birth rates remained high at least in the short run—and this represents the vast majority of the world—significant population growth was the result. One consequence in nineteenth-century Europe was emigration, often to the colonial world. But eventually birth rates came under control, and a slower rate of growth was achieved. In those places where birth rates came down relatively early, the history was somewhat different. France is virtually alone in this category. It took France a remarkably long time to go through its demographic transition. It began early and lasted a long time. Indeed, both fertility and mortality rates were declining among some groups as early as the second half of the eighteenth century. As fertility went down, age of last maternity generally came down as well, and particular populations experienced that decline more dramatically than others. From a benchmark of about 40 for last birth, the age came down to the mid-30s in the French middle class (lower in the aristocracy). One result later in the life course would be a longer period of time without children, one characteristic of old age.

England was experiencing declining death rates by 1800 and declining birth rates by the 1820s; they declined in parallel fashion over the course of the nineteenth century (Bardet and Dupâquier, T. 2, p. 12). The scholarship on fertility decline in the United States used to put it in the company of France, but now it appears that it paralleled Australia in experiencing fertility decline from the middle of the century. Transition in Germany and Italy came later in the nineteenth century, in Russia at its very end.

The first studies of the demographic transition paid much more attention to birth and death rates than anything else. Eventual declines in both rates constituted what has been called a vital revolution, a triumph of life over death. In the West, it began slowly around 1800, picking up speed in the late nineteenth century and achieving dramatic results with fertility and mortality declines in the four decades surrounding 1900. For a team of specialists on European historical demography, the "demographic revolution" ran from 1750 to 1914. More recently, with a focus on public health, medicine, and economic development, James Riley describes increasing life expectancy, the tendency to die in old age rather than childhood, and the shift in causes of death from infectious diseases to chronic ailments as a "health transition." His is a two-hundred-year history, from 1800 to 2000.

Despite the failure of large quantitative studies to confirm one model of demographic transition, historians have explored the experience of falling fertility in particular cultural settings. An important 1992 collection of studies of European fertility decline covers the period 1850–1970 but concentrates on 1890–1920, and it calls the process "the quiet revolution." It describes a world in which people practiced contraception of one sort or another. In the old demographic regime in western Europe, it had been late marriage, a limit on those who could marry, and a negligible number of births outside of marriage that kept population in control. With the transition, techniques of control ranged from coitus interruptus to the use of contraceptive devices. Associated with that shift came changes in relationships between husbands and wives and greater autonomy among women. Thus, demographic change was associated with if not caused by social and cultural change.

Demographers continue to attempt to paint a broad picture of long-term change; thus, Ronald Lee sees the "demographic transition" as a three-hundred-year process, still ongoing, from 1800 to 2100. In his view, no one has yet completed the transition, and the non-Western world at present is going through it faster than the West did historically. In discussing mortality, he points to preventive medicine, particularly with the discovery of a smallpox vaccine in the late eighteenth century, and the implementation of public health policies in the late nineteenth and twentieth centuries. Also important were the emergence of the germ theory of disease in the late nineteenth century and greater personal hygiene. Improved nutrition resulted from progress in the effectiveness of markets and storage of food.

Lee's version of the demographic transition reserves an important place for population aging. He builds upon the work of demographers who noticed that the age distribution of populations, what he calls "the last stage of the demographic transition," had changed along with birth and death rates. If the biggest overall change is the increase in the world's population, a significant part of the story has been the growing share of the aged. Thus, he writes,

Since 1800, global population size has already increased by a factor of six and by 2100 will have risen by a factor of ten. There will then be 50 times as many elderly, but only five times as many children; thus, the ratio of elders to children will have risen by a factor of ten.

(Lee, p. 167)

In the most fundamental way, it was falling fertility that gave rise to demographic aging, but there were also occasions when falling death rates in adulthood had a similar result. In the contemporary world, both factors have mattered. But at the start of the transition, declines in mortality clustered in early childhood. The impact at first would have been younger populations. But as the smaller birth cohorts grew up, populations aged, and for a long time it was fertility decline that caused population aging.

Those countries that experienced slow and steady fertility decline eventually saw slow and steady demographic aging. Some demographers, taking age 65 as the threshold of old age, measure the time it has taken a given country to double the percentage aged 65 and over from 7 to 14. The French experience ran for 115 years, from 1865 to 1980; for Sweden it ran for 85 years, from 1890 to 1975. The United States went through the process in 69 years, from 1944 to 2013, the United Kingdom 45 years, from 1930 to 1975. Japan, which has the distinction in the early twenty-first century of being the oldest population in the world, went through the process in only 26 years, from 1970 to 1996. China, which has experienced aging through its one-child policy, is expected to go through the process in the same time, but later, from 2000 to 2026. Developing countries can expect to go through the process even more quickly (Uhlenberg, p. 42).

We need not await the late twentieth and twenty-first centuries to observe meaningful aging. European countries, while not yet doubling the 65+ population, were already growing somewhat older in the late nineteenth and early twentieth centuries. Awareness of that development was accompanied by cultural fears. When the French tried to understand their defeat in the Franco-Prussian War of 1870–71, they compared their population to Germany's and identified military loss with lack of demographic dynamism. Henceforth, the social science of demography developed in a context of international strength and weakness. Falling fertility was seen as a serious national problem, and regime after regime began trying to boost birth rates. Demographers offered analysis and, in some cases, prescriptions for national revival, and awareness of the role of falling fertility in demographic aging led to a tendency to associate aged populations with national weakness.

We will return to the story of population aging when we reach the contemporary period and examine in greater detail the speed with which Asia and Latin America recapitulated in their own ways Western experiences of fertility decline. We will see that in international banking and development circles, which "normalized" the Western experience, this period is seen as an important opportunity during which temporarily enhanced working-age populations might boost production before the aging process catches up. We will also see that the discourse of decline that was evident in much of the Western world in the late nineteenth century would be repeated in the late twentieth. But we must also see how old age came to be seen as a social problem in the nineteenth-century West.

Works Cited and Further Reading

Jean-Pierre Bardet and Jacques Dupâquier, eds., *Histoire des populations de l'Europe*, T. 2 (Paris: Fayard, 1998); Jean-Claude Chesnais, *The Demographic Transition: Stages, Patterns, and Economic Implications. A Longitudinal Study of Sixty-Seven Countries Covering the Period 1720–1984* (Oxford: Clarendon Press, 1992); James C. Riley, *Rising Life Expectancy: A Global History* (Cambridge: Cambridge University Press, 2001); John R. Gillis, Louise A. Tilly, and David Levine, eds., *The European Experience of Declining Fertility, 1850–1970: The Quiet Revolution* (Cambridge, MA and Oxford: Blackwell, 1992); Ronald Lee, "The Demographic Transition: Three Centuries of Fundamental Change," *Journal of Economic Perspectives*, Vol. 17, No. 4 (Fall 2003): pp. 167–190; Peter Uhlenberg, ed., *International Handbook of Population Aging* (Dordrecht: Springer, 2009).

SECTION IV
Modernity and Old Age

8

FRAMING THE OLD PERSON AS PENSIONER AND OLD AGE AS A SOCIAL PROBLEM IN THE NINETEENTH AND EARLY TWENTIETH CENTURIES

In the previous chapter we examined the place of aging and the aged in the context of the demographic transitions. Here we focus on the ways in which older people became defined as pensioners and old age as constituting a social problem. Demographic facts and cultural representations make up part of the story, but we will look more closely at the emergence of social policy and both charitable and welfare institutions.

However, before addressing the emergence of pension programs designed to meet perceived social needs, we should recognize that some pensions were designed for relatively privileged older people. Civil servants even in the early modern era were rewarded with pensions, and they came to expect recognition of their contributions. Employees of the English customs and excise services, French tax farmers, and Austrian civil servants were among those singled out for support in retirement. They were rewarded for services rendered; they happened to be aging. To some extent, such support mirrored that provided to military veterans on both sides of the Atlantic, as even in the United States military pensions played an influential role. Civil War pensions have long been viewed as models for civilian pensions in the late nineteenth century, and economic historian Dora Costa estimates that they benefited a large number of northern White families, with beneficiaries including 35% of White males aged 55–59 as late as 1900 (Costa, p. 35). But there was earlier precedent in US history, as Revolutionary War pensions already supported a group of aging men. Retirement for civilians came later, as workforce participation by older Americans would not begin its gradual decline until the late nineteenth century.

The political rhetoric that emerged during the French Revolution evoked the desirability of providing a reward at the end of a career. Legislation calling for aid for the aged poor was not yet successfully implemented, but it was written, passed, and remembered in subsequent decades. Public sector functionaries were more successful in actually gaining pensions. Individual government ministries saw to their own employees even as regimes changed through cycles of revolution and reaction. By the middle of the nineteenth century, resources were combined for a whole range of ministries. Recipients might find themselves in need, but it would be hard to argue that they were always the neediest members of the population. What is remarkable is the emergence of formulas for rewarding careers that seem to anticipate pension and social security systems to come.

Bureaucrats in the French Revolutionary era earned pension rights, and soldiers continued to be awarded military pensions. Revolutionary rhetoric spoke about need and reward. Pensions were created under Napoleon as a way of ensuring adherence to his regime. And with the restoration of the Bourbon monarchy, elements of Revolutionary promise and Napoleonic policy survived. One population that has been studied over a relatively long period is magistrates in France from the late eighteenth century through the first half of the nineteenth. These individuals earned a positive right with 30 years of service and 60 years of age. Those who could claim such rights would be entitled to a pension based upon a formula of earnings in the last three years and total years of service. Other ministries followed suit, and funds were pooled. Other countries took their own paths. In England, by the 1850s, "the civil service pension was now almost, but not formally, a 'legal right'" (Thane, p. 241).

Most aging individuals were not so lucky. Indeed, for much of the nineteenth century, Enlightenment and Revolutionary-era ideals about social responsibility and welfare were abandoned. *Laissez-faire* capitalism and liberal individualism meant a retreat from state aid to every age group throughout Europe. Local governments and private charities tended to pay attention only to the very neediest, and individuals were left to their own devices. Nonetheless, workers with a tradition of craft or corporate organization began to imagine ways of addressing need in later life. Some formed friendly societies or mutual aid societies to pool resources and provide support for fellow members in time of emergency or, at the very least, to ensure proper burial. In England, almost half of the adult male population belonged to friendly societies in the mid-nineteenth century; two thirds did so in the 1870s (Thane, p. 194). This constituted voluntary insurance, not much to depend upon in old age. Historians have debated the effectiveness of poor relief. Thomson sees English poor relief as significant enough to compare it with later welfare-state provisions, but the most important survey of old age in English history argues, "Throughout the nineteenth century a large minority of old people received poor relief, but they often received very little, very late in life and grudgingly" (Thane, p. 171). Such help supplemented what old people could still earn from work or receive from family.

Although there was no great demographic aging in the last third of the nineteenth century, Western societies all moved towards providing increasing aid. They all became scandalized by the "discovery" of the indigent aged, those from poor and working-class backgrounds who had not benefited from an earlier cultural discovery of the more privileged elderly. They looked different, worn out by physical labor. Old age came to be defined as a social problem, public and private pensions emerged in various countries, and, as Thane puts it for England, the "'old-age pensioner' emerged as the archetypical older person" (p. 194). Christoph Conrad writes similarly of the importance of the pensioner in Germany, as does Elise Feller for early-twentieth-century France.

Pension legislation derived from several sources. They included traditional forms of poor relief that were now targeted towards older people, social scientific study of social questions, government investigations into the condition of the aged, and increasing awareness and abhorrence of the plight of aged individuals in workhouses. Overall, people began to recognize that arrangements such as the English Poor Law and friendly societies were insufficient to deal with what now appeared to be a problem.

Some social studies of the nineteenth century continue to be read by historians. Charles Booth's *The Life and Labour of the Poor in London* (1886) identified old-age poverty as the result of workers' incapacity. It was one of many studies that took social welfare out of the realm of moral judgment, and the author, like such notables as Alfred Marshall and Joseph Chamberlain, served on royal commissions investigating the aged poor. It became routine in Europe and the United States to see the workhouse as a source of stigma and a danger to be avoided.

Imagining ending up in reduced circumstances and compromised health led people in some Western countries to opt for one form or another of insurance. This presupposed a quantitative approach to life, including an awareness of rates of longevity. Timothy Alborn's history of life insurance in nineteenth-century Britain describes how the "sympathetic" life (a narrative of mortality and survival of vulnerable family members) combined with the "numbered" life (statistics of age and mortality), "medicalized" life (examination and certification), and "commodified" life (putting a price on life) to contribute to the growth of an increasingly important industry to deal with risk. While not primarily about old age, life insurance (much more common in Anglo-American society than in continental Europe) focused attention on age as a key variable, and Alborn's categories of life all applied in some measure to other forms of insurance, including what came to be called social insurance.

Social insurance was a way of expressing solidarity among people at risk. Otto von Bismarck offered social insurance for German workers in the 1880s. Separate legislation attended to health, workplace accident, and old age and invalidity insurance. Such programs were compulsory, but they were funded by employer and employee contributions. Older people who were still capable of working were expected to do so. The German system was essentially about income replacement for working men to avoid old-age poverty. Bismarck was attempting to gain worker support for an essentially conservative policy, and he had some success, but German workers also pushed for greater benefits through unions and parties of the left. Workers could be skeptical, as they had a sense of their own (and their parents') life expectancies and considered retirement as deferred compensation that might never be received.

Nevertheless, the Bismarck pensions made news across Europe, and each country focused on particular aspects of old-age poverty. Compared to Germany, Britain focused more on the very poor and women. Denmark created a plan with state money in 1891 but still included language of moral worthiness, ruling out those who had depended upon poor relief. New Zealand (1898), France (1905), and Great Britain (1908) eventually went further than Germany by moving away from worker contributions, but in each country, legislation developed in a step-by-step fashion. Thus, for example, the French granted pensions to the elderly poor in 1905 and to workers more generally in 1910. As in the United States, agricultural workers would receive benefits much later than their urban brethren. By 1911, more than a million people were receiving pensions in England. Sweden in 1913 set something of a standard by aiming for universal coverage in its non-contributory old age pensions, but British reforms in the 1920s moved back in the direction of worker contributions.

The French provinces of Alsace and Lorraine, which had become German territory as a result of the Franco-Prussian War of 1870–71, benefited from the Bismarck legislation. When they reverted to France as a result of the First World War, they maintained the German system of social legislation and remained distinct from the rest of France. Later in the twentieth century, the French system was more uniformly national, and questions of rights following the Second World War would be seen as universal. At that point the funding scheme had changed, from people's own contributions being invested and returned to transfers from those currently working to those retiring. Philosophically this meant a shift from individualism to intergenerational solidarity (Guerlain, p. 98).

Funds for sickness, accident, and old age developed in the second half of the nineteenth century in large industries, including mining and railroads. Occupational pensions spread to teachers and, eventually, people working in smaller enterprises. In a world of private and public pensions, retirement became something of a right that joined middle classes and working classes when they reached a particular age.

Historians who have written about these developments describe increasing acceptance of social rights and social solidarity to one degree or another. Each country has its own history, and within that history can be found a range of actors. Labor and Social Democratic parties were overcoming their traditional suspicion of pensions as deferred compensation. Agrarian parties, urban middle classes, and elites played roles in Scandinavian developments. Liberals in England borrowed ideas from Labor and, in the famous Beveridge report of 1942, spoke of "cradle to grave" social guarantees. In the immediate context of the 1940s, the welfare state could be seen as a reward for having put up with deprivation in the Great Depression and the Second World War. And such ideas appeared quickly in places that had been under British hegemony, South Africa and India for example. In the longer run, it was one of many examples of the emergence of social rights that followed the eighteenth- and nineteenth-century claims of civil and political rights. The British Labor government of Clement Atlee implemented the plan in 1945. Social conflicts continued, but increasingly there was agreement across much of the political spectrum that the needs of the aged had to be met. Still, women's pensions lagged well behind men's, especially if the women were benefiting as widows rather than as workers themselves. Even if their pensions were based upon their own work, lower wages and more discontinuous careers would result in smaller pensions.

Until the mid-twentieth century, different occupational and social groups often benefited differently from pension benefits within each country in the Western world. Greater uniformity would be achieved as the idea of the welfare state took hold. As has been suggested, lands in the wider world that had fallen under Western control and included large numbers of colonists came under some such provisions. Eventually, some segments of the colonized populations did too. We turn now to the global context.

Works Cited and Further Reading

Dora L. Costa, *The Evolution of Retirement: An American Economic History, 1880–1990* (Chicago: University of Chicago Press, 1998); John Resch, *Suffering Soldiers: Revolutionary War Veterans, Moral Sentiment, and Political Culture in the Early Republic* (Amherst: University of Massachusetts Press, 1999); Leslie Hannah, *Inventing Retirement: The Development of Occupational Pensions in Britain* (Cambridge: Cambridge University Press, 1986); William M. Graebner, *A History of Retirement: The Meaning and Function of an American Institution* (New Haven: Yale University Press, 1980). For the debate on workforce participation, see J.R. Moen, "The Supply and Demand for Retirement: Sorting out the Arguments," in K. Warner Schaie and W. Andrew Achenbaum, eds., *Societal Impact on Aging: Historical Perspectives* (NY: Spring 1993), pp. 74–82.

On the working out of Revolutionary-era promises, see Gilles Pollet and Bruno Dumons, *L'état et les retraites: Genèse d'une politique* (Paris: Belin, 1994). On an early development of a French pension system in the public sector, see David G. Troyansky, "Aging and Memory in a Bureaucratizing World: A French Historical Experience," in *Power and Poverty: Old Age in the Pre-Industrial Past*, edited by Susannah R. Ottaway, L.A. Botelho, and Katharine Kittredge (New York: Greenwood Press, 2002), pp. 15–30. On the English pension debate, see Pat Thane, *Old Age in English History: Past Experiences, Present Issues* (Oxford: Oxford University Press, 2000). On German and French pensions, see Christoph Conrad, *Vom Greis zum Rentner: Der Strukturwandel des Alters in Deutschland zwischen 1830 und 1930* (Göttingen: Vandenhoeck & Ruprecht, 1994), and Elise Feller, *Histoire de la vieillesse en France, 1900–1950* (Paris: Seli Arslan, 2005).

For a general introduction to social welfare history, see Young-sun Hong, "Social Welfare and Insurance," in *Encyclopedia of European Social History*, ed.,

Peter N. Stearns, Vol. 3 (NY: Charles Scribner's Sons, 2001), pp. 467–482. For the basics on the welfare state, see Steven M. Beaudoin, "The Welfare State," in *Encyclopedia of European Social History*, ed., Peter N. Stearns, Vol. 2 (NY: Charles Scribner's Sons, 2001), pp. 477–487.

For the importance of the workhouse, see Thane, *Old Age in English History*, and Carole Haber and Brian Gratton, *Old Age and the Search for Security: An American Social History* (Bloomington: Indiana University Press, 1994). On life insurance, see Timothy Alborn, *Regulated Lives: Life Insurance and British Society, 1800–1914* (Toronto: University of Toronto Press, 2009). For important changes in the structure of the French retirement system, see Laetitia Guerlain, "Vichy et les retraites: autour de la loi du 14 mars 1941 relative à l'allocation aux vieux travailleurs salariés," in Laetitia Guerlain and Hinda Hedhili, eds., *Vieillir à travers les âges: Retraites et dépendance* (Paris: Comité d'histoire de la sécurité sociale, 2013). For a view of the "Beveridge Revolution" as a gradual evolution, see John Macnicol, *The Politics of Retirement in Britain, 1878–1948* (Cambridge and NY: Cambridge University Press, 1998).

On gender and the welfare state, see Susan Pedersen, *Family, Dependence, and the Origins of the Welfare State: Britain and France, 1914–1945* (Cambridge: Cambridge University Press, 1993), Gisela Bock and Pat Thane, eds., *Maternity and Gender Policies: Women and the Rise of the European Welfare States, 1880s–1950s* (London: Routledge, 1991) and Seth Koven and Sonya Michel, eds., *Mothers of a New World: Maternalist Politics and the Origins of Welfare States* (NY: Routledge, 1993).

9

OLD AGE IN THE CONTEXT OF COLONIALISM, IMPERIALISM, AND DECOLONIZATION

One of the biggest unknowns in the history of aging is the impact of colonialism. The historiography of old age has been very Western, and the study of the non-Western world has commonly focused either on "traditional" representations of aging and the aged or on the contemporary challenge of demographic aging. Nonetheless, it is possible to sketch out a few broad characteristics and what might be undertaken in future research.

Globalization is sometimes presented as an innovation of the very recent past and an increasingly important feature of the contemporary world economy. Yet, historians know that trade and cultural exchange have characterized human history for a very long time. They also know that trade expanded and quickened in the early modern period and that as European states claimed colonies in the Americas, Asia, and Africa, new situations arose. The upending of patterns of local landholding and family work prompted changes for people at different ages of life, and market pressures would have encouraged individual rather than family-based economic decision-making. But how people negotiated these changes would have had a variety of consequences for the aged.

Histories of European "discoveries," settlement, and colonization are largely written from sources created by the conquerors. This is a hazardous enterprise. Some of the richest sources of information come from people who were trying to change the environments and people they found. Yet, sometimes the missionaries who were attempting to convert indigenous peoples created meticulous records of social and cultural practices. They may have been complicit with an effort to destroy, but they also felt an obligation to understand those they encountered, if only to know how better to convert them. This was true of the French in Canada, where there was a surprising degree of "going local," and of the Spanish in Mesoamerica. Let us say a word about the latter, for in that case we observe an encounter between highly developed civilizations. On the one hand, the urban Aztec culture dazzled the Spanish conquistadors; on the other hand, they were horrified by the practice of human sacrifice. Archaeological and pictorial remains provide some information, but some Spanish observers left detailed enough accounts to tell us something about the Aztec life course and, hence, old age.

Historian Caroline Dodds Pennock has relied heavily on the *Florentine Codex*, an account written between the 1540s and 1570s by Franciscan friar Bernardino of Sahagún, and the alphabetic and pictorial *Codex Mendoza*, which she accepts as an Indian product. The latter mentions old women as matchmakers and priestesses. The *Florentine Codex* refers to older women's sexuality outliving their husbands' (Pennock, p. 122), young men aging prematurely from illicit sexual activity (p. 140), and older men and women as passing "into a different realm as ancestral figures and guardians of tradition" (p. 160). The Dominican friar Diego Durán recounted the central role of elders in ceremonies honoring fallen warriors (pp. 158–159) and remarked upon the apparent respect shown the aged among the Aztecs:

> No nation on earth has held its elders in such fear and reverence as these people. The old father or mother was held in reverence under pain of death. Above all else these people charged their children to revere elders of any rank of social position. So it was that the priests of the law were esteemed, respected, by old and young, lord and peasant, rich and poor. Old people, in our own wretched times, are no longer honoured; they are held in contempt and are scorned.
>
> (p. 161)

Sahagún describes multiple ways in which older Aztecs functioned as educators and authority figures (pp. 162–163), but he also admits that eventually the old person would grow weaker and experience a "second childhood" (p. 165). It is in advanced age that the old person is allowed to drink alcohol, a concession to the long-honored but now diminished elder.

European travelers left their homes at young ages. The rigors of world trade often meant a return to Europe before the challenges of aging struck. For those who settled in the wider world, European patterns were adapted to local conditions. Accumulated wealth supported them in advanced age, and they built upon the cultural meanings they had carried with them. Thus, for example, colonial North America saw the development of ways of aging brought from across the Atlantic. While we don't yet have a study of aging to match Erik Seeman's *Death in the New World: Cross-Cultural Encounters, 1492–1800*, we can assume that ways of aging also involved curiosity about others' practices. Seeman's examination of "deathways" among Algonquian Indians, Akan-speaking slaves, Western European Jews, French Catholics, and English Protestants may serve as a model for such a study. His book demonstrates parallels among diverse peoples, and what we have seen in terms of cultural admonitions to respect elders suggests commonalities across time and space.

In those areas characterized by plantation labor, the intensification of work in the early modern period must have resulted in premature aging and death. Here and there we find hints of deference shown elders within individual groups. Historians speak of the respect shown older women in African American communities going back to the time of slavery. Leslie J. Pollard sees the importance of West African traditions and the support of the slave community as background to the development of African American experiences of aging. Elsewhere, there are suggestions of respect that crossed ethnic lines, whether shown American Indians, Asian elders, or aged African American slaves, but perhaps more important was the tendency on the part of European colonists to treat the colonized as children. The very language employed made such infantilization quite clear.

The idea of childlike non-Westerners is found not only in everyday speech but also in cultural representations that contrasted the maturity of the more developed world with the immaturity of other peoples. Thus, the metaphor of individual aging was applied to entire populations. Exceptions arose where Europeans recognized the ancient civilizations of India or China. Yet, even there, it was a simple matter to characterize those civilizations as having been degraded. And it was a simple rhetorical maneuver to claim that vital Europeans were needed to revive degraded others.

A key element in the spread of European power to the widest reaches of the world was the work of Christian missionaries. This meant the spread and appropriation of Christian ideas, but it also meant a challenge to indigenous beliefs. Thus, older religious authorities would find themselves in competition with often younger Western missionaries. The control of the sacred, so often seen as essential to the status of the aged, was up for grabs. And as increasing numbers of Westerners with more secular ideas followed, yet another challenge arose. The challenge would be institutionalized in Western forms of education.

The rhetoric of colonialism included various and often contradictory imaginings of the life course. The aging settler was presented as surrounded by youthful others. Or the young settler was bringing energy to a degraded culture. Rudyard Kipling may have recommended sending "the best ye breed" to "serve" the childish peoples of the wider world, but some proponents of colonialism thought it necessary to send weak young European men to discover their masculinity. Such an idea derived from the notion that modern civilization, particularly in the late nineteenth century, had become enervating. The debate certainly went back to the eighteenth century, when Philadelphia doctor Benjamin Rush seemed at least partly to take both sides, claiming that the percentage of the aged was greater in civilization than in the "savage nations" but that there was more death from disease among the civilized than among American Indians (Cassedy, p. 187). That might have been a surprise to the native peoples who had experienced huge rates of death from disease following contact with European colonists. Indeed, viruses carried by

Europeans had such a strong initial impact on American Indians between 15 and 40 that the very young and the old, who might have survived if provided some care by young adults, died of opportunistic secondary infections (Richter, pp. 60–61). Still, colonization provided opportunities for counting demographic events. European governments encouraged the keeping of quantitative records as a way of determining the strength of their overseas populations.

That is to take the point of view of the colonizer. What about the colonized? We may generalize about agrarian societies being overwhelmed by European intruders with technological power and a different sense of the calendar of life—indeed, the restructuring of landholding and agriculture would have meant another potential assault on the status of elders—but we may get at indigenous notions of aging through ethnographic study, oral traditions, memoirs, and literature of the colonial era. Let us consider some African examples.

Dominique Zahan, writing on sub-Saharan African thought, describes the high value placed on age. One achieves perfection only in old age, as full human status is only acquired in the last stage of life (Zahan, p. 21). One specialist on African childhood, Pierre Erny, describes the life course as a continuing process of perfection. One climbs a ladder and does not come back down (Erny, p. 23). Even when Amadou Hepâté Bá puts forth an idea of the African ladder of life, it peaks at 63, so the downhill steps, from 63 to 126, are beyond anything most people could hope for (Bá, *Aspects de la civilisation africaine*). That second phase was all about symmetry.

In North Africa as well we encounter ideas of a continuing process of maturation. One metaphor was that of the river and the water that comprised it. "It's not always the same water that flows, but it's always the same river" (Nasraoui, p. 18). Tunisian writer M.S. Mzali, recalls in her memoir, *Au fil de ma vie*, "Here I had arrived in old age with fewer illusions than at the start but with the same faith in the great principles" (p. 18). R. Mehl, in *Le vieillissement et la mort*, claims that it's in old age that man "seals a work that he began upon reaching maturity" (p. 19).

Ethnographers still see age, generation, and kinship structures as essential ways of understanding African societies and traditions. The Western sociological model of three ages—formation, work, and retirement—makes little sense, and Manga Bekombo writes that in Africa there are no old people, only "elders." That is to say that aging people play a prominent role whether as chiefs of communities, heads of families, or masters of cult, resources, and knowledge. Seemingly the arrivals of Islam and Christianity did little to change such matters in any fundamental way. As Bekombo explains, the African life course can be understood as consisting of five stages, linking the aging individual to a kind of eternity: before birth, childhood, adulthood, old age, after death (Bekombo, p. 120). According to Leopold Rosenmayr, traditional Bambara philosophy used the old tree to symbolize the position of the elder, from clan and village to social and mythical universe. To grow old, thus, is to grow ("Postface: Vieillir c'est grandir," p. 344).

The great African epic of *Sundiata*, whose events purport to reach back to the thirteenth century, describes the public whipping of respectable elders as a particularly heinous crime. In one version of the epic, we encounter a proverb that uses a rock to symbolize the elder. "When the egg falls on the rock, it's the egg that breaks; when the rock falls on the egg, it's even worse!" (Camara Laye, *Le maître de la parole*, cited in Grosskreutz, p. 23). As another proverb puts it, proclaiming the wisdom of the aged: "Even when staying seated, the old person sees what the standing adolescent cannot" (Amar Samb, *Matraqué par le destin*, cited in Grosskreutz, p. 25).

Griots or storytellers were often aged themselves, but even when they weren't they told stories that were rich in elderly characters who made their way into print both in collections of oral tradition and in colonial-era novels. In Senegal, for example, French colonizers began producing novels of colonization in the 1920s, but by the 1930s Western-educated Africans were adapting the novel to their purposes, peopling their own works with strong elders who recalled local proverbs and used biting repartee to comment on contemporary affairs. They spoke for African traditions and norms. And while they might have collaborated early on with the colonizers, they quickly spoke for their own people facing ideas and technologies coming from afar. As West Africans moved toward independence, writing in Senegal and Mali took on a new task, reminding younger people, especially those who favored change and exercised a new kind of political authority, of how things used to be. They represented the culture, wisdom, and dignity of Africa before colonization. The old character attempted to defend his or her culture, doing the work that African-born historians were also doing on matters of history and identity.

Colonial conquest and settlement were represented as rejuvenating Western conquerors and settlers. They were related as well to ideas of warfare as strengthening the masculinity of the nation. The rhetoric of warfare had little room for the elderly except as victims and dependents. Yet, the First World War raised the possibility of veterans' pensions. Memory of military glory and suffering would be accompanied by financial support. As European armies enlisted colonized Africans and Asians, the population of war pensioners became increasingly diverse. When non-European veterans found that their pensions were not the equal of Europeans' they protested and had to ponder the degree to which they "belonged" in states for which they had fought. Historical research on those veterans has only begun but includes studies of African soldiers fighting for France in the First World War and surviving in the subsequent decades.

The First World War was crucial in the development of veterans' pensions, but South Africans already debated the needs of aged veterans after the Anglo-Boer War (1899–1902). *Oudstryders* or old soldiers on the Boer side were the object of discussion. By the 1920s, civil pensions were on the South African agenda. The Social Pension Act of 1928 put in place a non-contributory, means-tested program for White South Africans. Discussion of the "deserving poor" followed in the tradition of nineteenth-century European social policy, but Blacks and Indians were left out until 1944, when they were brought into the system, and South Africa offered the first such assistance on the continent, followed by Equatorial Guinea in 1947 and Burundi in 1956 (Sagner, pp. 523–553). It is thought that the reformism of the early 1940s constituted an attempt to hasten national integration in time of war, but scholars also identify the ideas expressed in the Atlantic Charter of 1941 and the Beveridge Report of 1942 as encouraging South African reform. Worldwide expectations were growing out of the experience of world war.

It is worth considering not only when political movements and governments initiated pensions and other social reforms but also how recipients viewed them. Even though Blacks received smaller amounts than Whites, they saw what they did receive as rooted in right rather than privilege or gift. The government had claimed to replace paternalist chiefs, and the provision of aid in old age came to be seen as a moral obligation. One might even see the emergence of some kind of "common humanity" bridging racial differences as far as the aged are concerned, but the postwar apartheid regime expressed hostility to such an idea. Still, with the receipt of modest pensions, Blacks made them an important part of their family budgets. Ever since the late nineteenth century, significant numbers of Black laborers migrated for work, and "traditional" life course patterns and intergenerational relations were changed. Pensions were increasingly important. Oral histories collected in the 1990s revealed memories of mid-century change. One Mrs. F.X. recounted in 1997:

> When my grandparents got the pension money everything changed completely. Before that we had nothing. We were starving. My grandparents had nothing. But then they got the money. It helped us to survive. Before that it was not nice to be old. It is much better now than it used to be.
> *(Sagner, p. 546)*

In a sense, the granting of pensions meant that elders weakened by the modern labor market could now exercise some authority. Grandparents could play a central role. Women's position was strengthened, as men with a small number of cattle were deemed too wealthy to merit a pension. But pension money tended to be pooled, and rural traders were immediately aware of families' resources.

A study of aging Tunisians reveals a similar appreciation of pensions. Amira Bournaz, in *C'était Tunis 1920, récit de vie*, recalls the difference education, employment, and retirement made in her life.

> At present at the end of my life, whenever I receive my retired public official's pension, I bless my mother in her grave, I thank her for having given me an education, a stable job and a retirement pension. I'm not dependent on anyone thanks to her.
> *(Bournaz, pp. 39–40, cited in Nasraoui, p. 38)*

If we look ahead to the experience of decolonization, we may see parallels with the representations of age in revolutionary and post-revolutionary societies of the West. We might find youthful individuals breaking with an oppressive past, whether that of the European colonizer or of the older independence leader, as in the young Tunisian militant movement that broke in 1934 from the old leaders of the Constitutional Party. They distinguished themselves from the "vain phraseologies" of their elders (Nasraoui, p. 22). The reforming New Culture Movement in China (ca. 1915–1927) advocated the prioritization of youth over age. One of its leaders, Chen Duxiu, launched a political/literary journal, *New Youth*, in 1915, calling for a turn towards science and democracy. A more extreme case for prioritizing youth over age came in the Cultural Revolution (1966–1975), when political leaders accused older party cadres of counter-revolutionary thinking. But even a new society might eventually be characterized by aging revolutionaries' leadership. The Russian and Chinese Revolutions involved dramatic land reforms that had an impact on intergenerational relations. For millions of people, rapid political change meant growing old in a world very different from the one in which they had grown up. However, revolutionary regimes could use elders as bearers of memories of past injustice, and revolutionary parties had a tendency to become bureaucratized, in some places and at some times appearing gerontocratic. Elements of traditional culture, such as Confucianism and coresidence of aged parents and adult children in China, had a way of continuing to play important roles, as elders maintained some status in rural and urban China in the post-Revolutionary decades. The pattern would occur differently around the world, but representations of a youthful Mao, Gandhi, Kenyatta, Mandela, or Castro would give way to more mature images in power. How they played out in memory would be worth exploring.

A new history of aging, colonialism, and decolonization, something that has not yet been written, would look at local situations to understand the life course of the colonist, between old world and new. It would encompass traditional and evolving representations of age among the colonized, whether in village or urban society or among elites and intermediaries. It would tease out attitudes and behavior of historical actors in their homes, places of work, and institutions of government, administration, and assistance. Rather than try to generalize about confrontations between supposedly unchanging Confucianism, Hinduism, or Islam with Western Christianity, it would examine particular circumstances and lifeways. It would not simply skip from classical texts to the demographic challenges of the contemporary world, but it would recognize more complicated and long-term interactions and migrations. Models of such study may be found in social-science literature on comparative aging. To take one early example, anthropologist Charlotte Ikels compared Chinese diasporas in Hong Kong and Boston, where Confucian ideals operated differently, as did residential patterns, neighborhood dynamics, systems of transportation, and social interactions. For Ikels, it was a question of aging and adaptation. Historians of aging, recognizing that Confucian ideals have been modified to suit modern conditions, might pay more attention to such complexities in earlier periods and in other lands.

One possible approach that is only beginning to take shape is to look at medical thought and practice, but so far the literature on colonizers and colonized has paid much more attention to childhood, youth, gender, sexuality, and approaches to particular diseases than to aging and the aged. We will explore the emergence of geriatrics as a specialty in chapter 12, but it is worth recalling here that even in the ancient and medieval periods there were parallels and intersections among the traditions of Mediterranean, South Asian, and Chinese medicine. All were humoral, with Galen identifying four humors (yellow bile, black bile, phlegm, and blood), South Asian physicians recognizing three (phlegm, bile, and wind), and the Chinese counting six. All prescribed maintaining equilibrium among the humors. In Europe the Galenic model was challenged in the early modern period and more thoroughly by biomedicine in the nineteenth century. But even as Europeans privileged biomedicine in the era of High Imperialism, other traditions coexisted. Some scholars have spoken of resistance. Others emphasize alternative or complementary systems, as some colonizers were drawn to local practices and some of the colonized opted selectively for cosmopolitan medicine. Historians of Unani (Indo-Muslim) medicine see vitality and creativity in that tradition long past the arrival of the British in India. Ayurveda and Chinese Traditional Medicine became associated with Indian and Chinese nationalisms, but patients chose from a range of possibilities. And in the present significant minorities of European and North American patients choose from a variety of "Eastern" practices, sometimes accompanied by "new-age" philosophies. At the very same time, residents of "Chinatowns" and other immigrant communities combine traditional and cosmopolitan medicine. Even bodily experiences of aging, or at least ways of describing bodily experiences, vary from population to population. For example, American and European women tend to identify midlife transition with menopause and have sometimes opted for hormone replacement therapy; in China, the midlife transition (*Gengnianqi*) is associated more with irritability and anger, not the cessation of menstruation per se, and in Japan the transition is associated with bodily aches (Shea).

Different ways of understanding the aging body and different ways of treating it coexist in a postcolonial world. Such is the legacy of the history of colonialism, decolonization, and migration. But migration often involves movement between very different state systems, and those systems set different rules for dealing with and sometimes paying for the infirmities and accidents of life. We now turn to the state.

Works Cited and Further Reading

For one example of the problem of understanding the non-Western intellectual world on the eve of colonization, see Sheldon Pollock, ed., *Forms of Knowledge in Early Modern Asia: Explorations in the Intellectual History of India and Tibet, 1500–1800* (Durham: Duke University Press, 2011). For the Aztecs, see Caroline Dodds Pennock, *Bonds of Blood: Gender, Lifecycle and Sacrifice in Aztec Culture* (Houndmills, Basingstoke, Hampshire, England and NY: Palgrave Macmillan, 2008). On

North America, see Erik Seeman, *Death in the New World: Cross-Cultural Encounters, 1492–1800* (Philadelphia: University of Pennsylvania Press, 2010); Leslie J. Pollard, *Complaint to the Lord: Historical Perspectives on the African American Elderly* (Selinsgrove, PA: Susquehanna University Press, 1996); James H. Cassedy, *Demography in Early America: Beginnings of the Statistical Mind, 1600–1800* (Cambridge: Harvard University Press, 1969); Daniel K. Richter, *Facing East from Indian Country: A Native History of Early America* (Cambridge, MA: Harvard University Press, 2001).

Dominique Zahan, *Religion, spiritualité et pensée africaines* (Paris: Payot, 1970); Pierre Erny, *L'enfant et son milieu en Afrique noir* (Paris: Payot, 1972); Amadou Hepâté Bá, *Aspects de la civilisation africaine* (Paris: Présence africaine, 1972); Camara Laye, *Le maître de la parole* (Paris: Plon, 1978); and Amar Samb, *Matraqué par le destin* (Dakar: Nouvelles éditions africaines, 1973) are all cited in Béatrice Grosskreutz, *Le personnage de l'ancien dans le roman sénégalais et malien de l'époque colonial: Un élément de continuité culturelle dans un univers ébranlé* (Frankfurt: Verlag für Interkulturelle Kommunikation, 1993). Mustapha Nasraoui, *La vieillesse dans la société tunisienne* (Paris: L'Harmattan, 2003), in which M.S. Mzali, *Au fil de ma vie* (Tunis : Editions H.M., 1972), R. Mehl, *Le vieillissement et la mort* (Paris : PUF, 1962), and Amira Bournaz, *C'était Tunis 1920, récit de vie* (Tunis : Cerés Ed., 1993) are all cited. Translations are mine. Manga Bekombo, "Vieillissement, culture et société en Afrique," and Léopold Rosenmayr, "Postface: Vieillir c'est grandir," in Claudine Attias-Donfut and Léopold Rosenmayr, eds., *Vieillir en Afrique* (Paris: PUF, 1994).

Richard Fogarty, *Race and War in France: Colonial Subjects in the French Army, 1914–1918* (Baltimore: Johns Hopkins University Press, 2008); Gregory Mann, *Native Sons: West African Veterans and France in the Twentieth Century* (Durham, NC: Duke University Press, 2006); Andreas Sagner, "Ageing and Social Policy in South Africa: Historical Perspectives with Particular Reference to the Eastern Cape," *Journal of Southern African Studies*, Vol. 26, No. 3 (Sep. 2000): 523–553.

Deborah Davis-Friedmann, *Long Lives: Chinese Elderly and the Communist Revolution* (Cambridge, MA: Harvard University Press, 1983); Charlotte Ikels, *Aging and Adaptation: Chinese in Hong Kong and the United States* (Hamden, CT: Archon Books, 1983). On medicine in the colonial context, see Megan Vaughan, *Curing their Ills: Colonial Power and African Illness* (Cambridge, UK: Polity Press, 1991). On Unani medicine, see Seema Alavi, *Islam and Healing: Loss and Recovery of an Indo-Muslim Medical Tradition, 1600–1900* (Basingstoke: Palgrave Macmillan, 2008), and Claudia Liebeskind, "Unani Medicine of the Subcontinent," in *Oriental Medicine: An Illustrated Guide to the Asian Arts of Healing*, edited by Jan Van Alphen and Anthony Aris (London: Serindia Publications, 1995), pp. 39–64. On different ways of understanding the aging body, see Jeanne L. Shea, "Venting Anger From the Body During *Gengnianqi*: Meanings of Midlife Transition Among Chinese Women in Reform-Era Beijing," Chapter Three in *Transitions and Transformations: Cultural Perspectives on Aging and the Life Course*, edited by Caitrin Lynch and Jason Danely (NY and Oxford: Berghahn Books, 2013).

10

AGING AND THE WELFARE STATE

The welfare state, which one economic historian describes as "an attempt to influence the *distribution and stability of individual life chances of the total population*" (Flora, p. 13), began as a largely European phenomenon, with important parallels, offshoots, and occasional precursors in North America and settler colonies around the world. New Zealand and Australia pioneered some elements, but European welfare states offered what became standard models for dealing with social risk across the life course in much of the world. As far as the aged are concerned, European welfare states tried to ensure minimal standards of living, with pensions seen as a reward after many years of work. Eventually, world populations would share comparable institutional arrangements and late-life expectations. This chapter focuses on policies and problems that emerged in the West in particular economic and demographic circumstances and then spread elsewhere.

European legislation clustered around the turn of the twentieth century, with emphasis on social insurance and pensions. Early welfare state institutions were characterized by the sharing of risk. As contributions by workers were supplemented or replaced by state funds, the welfare state increasingly orchestrated the transfer of income. The primary beneficiaries were urban factory workers; rural workers lagged behind. The early history of social security systems and welfare states emphasized new norms for dealing with poverty and setting basic expectations for the human life course, but old age policy evolved into something much more universal. An important tipping point in favor of the welfare state came as benefits began to accrue to middle-class people. Even the Scandinavian welfare states, which are often seen as the classic social-democratic examples, came into being through the support of middle-class and agrarian political parties. Acceptance of a shared experience of old age came in the aftermath of the Second World War. In terms of replacement of income, the high point came from the 1950s to the 1970s. Then came a period of economic downturn, with a generalized critique of welfare-state assumptions beginning in the 1980s, but benefits grew for many, and beneficiaries saw them as a matter of right. Meanwhile, the characteristic elements of the welfare state spread to such places as East Asia and South America, where demographic experiences and economic realities were different.

Demographic aging in the late nineteenth century provided the context for experiments in New Zealand and Australia, where very young populations had previously been the norm. Earlier in the century, New Zealanders set up a welfare system relying upon family support. The 1846 Destitute Persons Ordinance made no mention of community support, as individuals and families were to take care of themselves and each other. It was a far cry from the English Poor Law tradition of community care. That changed with the 1898 Old Age Pensions Act. Even though revisions of the 1846 Ordinance still emphasized family responsibilities, now there would be a right to assistance by non-relatives, "non-contributory pensions for the general citizenry past age 65" (Thomson, "Old Age in the New World," p. 160). Australia also went from a youthful population of immigrants to the aging of "goldrush generations" at a time of economic depression in the 1890s. The aged had been few and far between in 1850s Australia, "a society without grandparents" (Davison, p. 40). In cultural terms, youthful Australia contrasted with "old Mother Britain" (p. 41). But aging and depression revealed a new sort of dependence. As Graeme Davison puts it,

> The idea that the nation's old folks were entitled to the support of the State because of their pioneering contribution to the development of the country was the moral basis on which the colonies of Victoria (1899) New South Wales (1900) and Queensland (1907) and later the Commonwealth (1908) were to enact non-contributory schemes for Old Age Pensions. These measures expressed a strong consensus that the old age pension, so far from being a form of charitable relief, was a kind of deferred reward for past services.
>
> (p. 47)

Yet, Pat Jalland's new history of old age in Australia, which includes compelling descriptions of individual men and women, sees the elderly as being "forgotten" after 1908 and once again receiving attention only in the 1940s and after, when considerable thought, beyond matters of economic and health needs, went into the design of housing for the aged.

Rewarding past service is one way of understanding the creation of old age pensions and the welfare state of which they form a part, but they coexist with other explanations. They might involve dealing with current emergencies, they might have something to do with ideas of changing needs across the life course, they might involve ideals of intergenerational altruism, and they might have something to do with employer–employee contracts (Denis Kessler, "But Why Is There Social Security?"). Whatever the explanation, discussions of the needs of the elderly extended across national boundaries and resulted in comparable mechanisms. They were a function of industrial and post-industrial development, social conflicts, perceived old-age poverty, and broad acceptance of the role of the state in providing old-age security. But before the state became the dominant player, private-sector companies played a role, and individual colonial governments in Australia and state governments in the United States made important contributions.

A debate exists about why aging workers began leaving the workforce at the turn of the nineteenth to twentieth century. Some historians of Britain and the United States see economic, technological, and workforce management issues (Macnicol; Graebner); others see some improved opportunities (Costa, among others). But the trickle toward retirement became a bigger movement as the twentieth century wore on. In the American "Social Security Era," the context for old age pensions shifted from the private to the public sphere (Haber and Gratton, pp. 181–185) and from individual states to the federal government. Two years before the passage of the Social Security Act of 1935, which addressed both needy elders and young workers trying to avoid future poverty, 21 states plus Alaska and Hawaii already had programs to deal with old-age relief, and the popular ideas of Upton Sinclair, Huey Long, and Francis Townsend made old-age poverty a widespread topic of discussion (Achenbaum, "Public Pensions," pp. 116–118). The most recent study of the Townsend Plan and the movement of its supporters sees its continued importance even after the passage of the Social Security Act and lessons for movement politics more generally (Amenta). But the shift to the public sphere was not so simple. Steven Sass speaks of "the heyday of private pensions," which he locates as simultaneous with the welfare state. Such pensions were achieved and maintained through collective bargaining, with the model being set in the very period we normally associate with the triumph of social security after the Second World War. Such major unions as the United Mine Workers and the United Auto Workers played a key role, and federal support was assured when, in 1948–1949, the National Labor Relations Board ruled and the Supreme Court confirmed that pensions were "within the statutory scope of collective bargaining" (Sass, p. 100). The 1949 Steel Industry Board report spoke of "social obligation" to supplement what the government provided, and the report's idea, along with the power of the strike, formed the background to the "Memorandum of Agreement on Retirement and Health and Security Programs" between Ford and the UAW.

Private sector employers in an American economy that traditionally emphasized free-market solutions nonetheless came to welcome the government's taking on new responsibilities, and some of them, wanting to see superannuated workers depart the workplace, saw real benefit in combining private and public pensions. Thus, changes in workforce management played some role. The Great Depression and the Second World War formed the background to American welfare-state development, but the process took time. The Depression made it difficult to pay benefits, and the Social Security Act in the US wouldn't have widespread impact on retirement until later. The Second World War marks the general divide, but important amendments that truly secured Social Security in American political culture only came in 1950.

Every nation had its own experience, with a different blend of universal or means-tested benefits for each occupation, marital status, and sex. Overall, however, there was a general acceptance of a right to a secure old age. And the political development occurred just as populations were about to enter a phase of rapid demographic aging.

Sweden serves as the classic example of the European welfare state. In the earliest period, 1890–1930, it consisted of comprehensive social assistance and insurance plans whose benefits were somewhat minimal. Then, in 1930–1960, it developed into a national safety net to provide adequate support for all. From 1960 until late in the twentieth century, Swedish elderly received generous benefits, with small towns and rural areas catching up to cities and the state taking over financial responsibility that had previously been in the hands of families. Similarly, most European programs date from the turn of the twentieth century, with significant growth in entitlements in the decades following the Second World War. Attempts to scale back programs came in the last decades of the twentieth century.

One of the major questions for all countries was whether to fund retirement pensions through general revenues or contributions from workers' salaries. The English welfare state saw a shift in the 1920s to a contributory system. Pat Thane argues that that decade saw "the establishment of the framework on which the system was built for the remainder of the century," that the post-Second World War legislation was less about framework and functioning than about universality (Thane, p. 327). Demographers, economists, politicians, and eugenicists paid serious attention to demographic aging in the 1930s and 1940s, but by the 1950s there was less of a panic about aging, at least until the 1980s. What was becoming clear in England and the rest of the Western world was a decline in workforce participation by the aged. By the 1930s, the Great Depression accentuated the long-term pattern, and most elderly men found themselves out of work, but the tendency continued even as the world economy recovered and achieved unparalleled prosperity. Thane refers to census data of the percentage of Englishmen over the age of 65 in paid work:

1881	73
1901	65
1931	48
1951	31
1961	23
1971	19
1980	13

Thirteen percent of women over 60 were in paid work in 1901, only five percent in 1951. Thus, gender distinctions remained, but some historical trends operated in parallel fashion.

The decrease in workforce participation by older adults appears to be relatively steady across the twentieth century, but it took a while for people's expectations to catch up with the trend. People came to recognize an important shift from full-time employment to full-time inactivity after the Second World War. In England, white-collar workers had already grown used to retirement between the world wars; blue-collar workers joined them after the Second World War.

Throughout the Western world, old age was increasingly associated with retirement and rights to security. This cut across class lines. Sociologists looking back at the middle decades of the twentieth century speak of the normalization of a life course characterized by three periods: training, work, and retirement (Kohli). The idea was that retirement corresponded to the threshold of old age.

In the middle decades of the twentieth century, the direction of change was fairly linear, as benefits became increasingly universal and gender distinctions, while continuing to exist, became somewhat less pronounced. In western Europe, "cradle to grave" benefits came to be seen as rights that were difficult to envision losing. But even as new norms and entitlements seemed secure, some, particularly on the political right, called them into question. At the same time, scholars began to notice that in the most advanced welfare states the structure of training/work/retirement, with retirement corresponding to old age, had begun to come apart in the 1970s and 1980s. According to sociologist Anne-Marie Guillemard, there was a challenge to the "threefold model of the life course," "dechronologizing" and "deinstitutionalizing" it (Guillemard, p. 165). People were leaving the workforce long before they would become eligible to receive pensions (p. 170). There were "other welfare subsystems": "unemployment compensation and disability insurance" (p. 171). In Europe, different parts of the welfare state were providing benefits in late adulthood or early old age. In the United States, some private companies were encouraging early withdrawal. In both contexts, according to Guillemard, "employability" was being defined in economic rather than medical terms; old age was being defined more functionally than chronologically (p. 173). As she writes,

> The aging worker is no longer primarily someone said to be close to the age of entitlement to retirement; instead, he is defined as being unable to work. When, as in West Germany or the Netherlands, nearly half of those who reach retirement age have previously been managed by disability insurance programmes, economic activity no longer means having the right to rest; it means being unfit for work.
>
> *(p. 174)*

Western societies in the late twentieth century were growing more "flexible," but the flexibility was seen to advantage employers rather than employees, and, after a few decades of predictable retirements, the tide seemed to be turning, as occupational old age was now preceding retirement and physical old age (pp. 177–178). An important element of the public debate in the 1980s was whether it would be necessary to make major cuts to welfare state benefits, to means-test them and to abandon universality. Such ideas were attractive on the right. Yet, even in Great Britain and the United States in that decade, Margaret Thatcher and Ronald Reagan's policies could not eliminate their countries' systems of social security, particularly as they applied to the aged. It became evident that middle-class voters cherished old-age benefits. Late-twentieth-century ideas of privatization led many large employers in the United States to shift their employees from "deferred-benefit" pension plans to "defined-contribution" programs that created greater risk for individuals. Some of those who opposed maintenance of the welfare state looked for inspiration to experiments with individual savings in Chile, but that turned out to be a short-lived model.

Some of the late-twentieth-century discussions explored the philosophical grounds of public policy. They tried to make sense of generational experiences and intergenerational responsibilities, solidarities, and conflicts. In looking at practical politics, they posited an inevitable "crisis" of the welfare state and suggested that the "golden age of pensions" could not be sustained. As David Thomson has put it, debates about the welfare state's redistribution policies were less and less about rich and poor, more and more about generations (Thomson, "The Welfare State and Generation Conflict"). And while those generations could be theorized in abstract ways, or in terms of the experiences most people in the modern and post-modern worlds could expect, it was increasingly tempting to identify generations more concretely as Depression-era, boomer, post-boomer, etc. In that mode of thinking, it was possible to speak of a social-security generation and winners and losers. Those who benefited most could be seen as a "selfish" generation; their children and grandchildren might be seen as having little chance of benefiting so well. Thus, intergenerational conflict came to characterize some policy debates.

All of this happened very quickly. It hadn't been for long that the vast majority of citizens of the developed world could expect a secure retirement and old age. As geographer Françoise Cribier discovered, cohorts born before and after the First World War, retiring respectively in 1972 and 1984, had very different expectations and experiences of retirement. The younger cohort was healthier, wealthier, and more capable of having a plan for retirement. So just as the broader working population of France grew accustomed to a secure Third Age, politicians in the Anglo-American world were calling it into question. Moreover, as Guillemard and other sociologists had discovered, economic pressures were pushing people into earlier retirements. Thane writes that in England the first cohort after 1945 experienced retirement as a shock while retirees in the 1960s and 1970s had a greater understanding and appreciation of what retirement could be (Thane, pp. 405–406).

Thus, the last decades of the twentieth century saw what seemed to be the full bloom of old age security along with economic and demographic challenges to it. Flexibility and individualism seemed to announce an important shift. Yet, the welfare state model was important in global debates about aging and the life course. When, in the aftermath of the Second World War, Japan sought to rebuild its economy, welfare-state measures and social security programs were not high on the agenda. But, with European and American models before it, Japan turned seriously toward such policies in the 1970s. Ninety percent of households were covered by eight pension programs: Employees' Pension (private firms), People's Pension (self-employed, including farmers), Seamen's Pension, National Government Employees' Pension, Local Government Employees' Pension, Public Corporations Employees' Pension, Private Schools Employees' Pension, and Agricultural Corporations Employees' Pension. As in the West, while the public thought benefits came from accumulated contributions, they were actually intergenerational transfers.

Japan fell between the large public sector in Europe and private models in the US. But the condition of the aged was different from both, as Japan made the cultural choice of a much higher rate of coresidence with children than in either of the other places. Indeed, Japan was closer to India and other Asian countries in that way. In the next chapter we will see how, in the face of Western models of aging and retirement, other experiences developed in the wider world.

Works Cited and Further Reading

Peter Flora, "On the History and Current Problems of the Welfare State," in *The Welfare State and its Aftermath*, edited by S.N. Eisenstadt and Ora Ahimeir (Totowa, NJ: Barnes and Noble Books, 1985); Steven M. Beaudoin, "The Welfare State," in *Encyclopedia of European Social History*, ed., Peter N. Stearns, Vol. 2 (NY: Charles Scribner's Sons, 2001), pp. 477–487; Abram de Swaan, *In Care of the State: Health Care, Education, and Welfare in Europe and the USA in the Modern Era* (NY: Oxford University Press, 1988); Peter Baldwin, *The Politics of Social Solidarity: Class Bases of the European Welfare State, 1875–1975* (Cambridge and NY: Cambridge University Press, 1990); David Thomson, "Old Age in the New World: New Zealand's Colonial Welfare Experiment," in Paul Johnson and Pat Thane, eds., *Old Age: from Antiquity to Postmodernity* (London and NY: Routledge, 1998); Graeme Davison, "'Our Youth is Spent and our Backs are Bent': the Origins of Australian Ageism," in *Australian Cultural History*, 14 (1995): 40–62; Pat Jalland, *Old Age in Australia: A History* (Melbourne: Melbourne University Press, 2015); Denis Kessler, "But Why Is There Social Security?" chapter 5 in *Workers Versus Pensioners: Intergenerational Justice in an Ageing World*, edited by Paul Johnson, Christoph Conrad, and David Thomson (Manchester and NY: Manchester University Press, 1989).

John Macnicol, *The Politics of Retirement in Britain, 1878–1948* (Cambridge and NY: Cambridge University Press, 1998); William M. Graebner, *A History of Retirement: The Meaning and Function of an American Institution* (New Haven: Yale University Press, 1980); Dora L. Costa, *The Evolution of Retirement: An American Economic*

History, 1880–1990 (Chicago: University of Chicago Press, 1998); Carole Haber and Brian Gratton, *Old Age and the Search for Security: An American Social History* (Bloomington: Indiana University Press, 1994); W. Andrew Achenbaum, "Public Pensions as Intergenerational Transfers in the United States," chapter 7 in *Workers Versus Pensioners*; Edwin Amenta, *When Movements Matter: The Townsend Plan and the Rise of Social Security* (Princeton: Princeton UP, 2006). Steven Sass, "Pension Bargains: The Heyday of US Collectively Bargained Pension Arrangements," chapter 6 in *Workers Versus Pensioners*.

Richard B. Freeman, Robert H. Topel, and Birgitta Swedenborg, editors, *The Welfare State in Transition: Reforming the Swedish Model* (Chicago: University of Chicago Press, 1997), particularly chapter 5: Thomas Aronsson and James R. Walker, "The Effects of Sweden's Welfare State on Labor Supply Incentives"; Pat Thane, *Old Age in English History: Past Experiences, Present Issues* (Oxford: Oxford University Press, 2000); Martin Kohli, "The World We Forgot: A Historical Review of the Life Course," in V.W. Marshall, ed., *Later Life: The Social Psychology of Aging* (Beverly Hills, CA: Sage, 1986), pp. 271–303; Anne-Marie Guillemard, "The Trend Towards Early Labour Force Withdrawal and the Reorganization of the Life Course: A Cross-national Analysis," chapter 9 in *Workers Versus Pensioners*; David Thomson, "The Welfare State and Generation Conflict: Winners and Losers," chapter 3 in *Workers Versus Pensioners*; Françoise Cribier, "Changes in Life Course and Retirement in Recent Years: The Example of Two Cohorts of Parisians," chapter 10 in *Workers Versus Pensioners*; see also her "Changes in the Experiences of Life between Two Cohorts of Parisian Pensioners, born in circa 1907 and 1921," in *Ageing and Society* (2005): 637–654; Naomi Maruo, "The Development of the Welfare Mix in Japan," and Yukio Noguchi, "Overcommitment in Pensions: The Japanese Experience," both in *The Welfare State East and West*, edited by Richard Rose and Rei Shiratori (New York and Oxford: Oxford University Press, 1986).

SECTION V
Globalizing, Medicalizing, and Disciplining Old Age

11

AGING IN A GLOBAL CONTEXT

In both demographic aging and the construction of welfare-state measures for dealing with support of the aged, the West had the earliest experiences, offering the rest of the world both models and cautionary tales. Population aging in the Western world varied from country to country but collectively took a relatively long time when compared with the experiences of other regions. In western Europe, the doubling of those 65 and over took 50–115 years. Elsewhere, it has taken 20–30. Welfare states, with their immediate origins in the nineteenth century, developed fully in the West in the second half of the twentieth century. Elsewhere, they developed partially and fitfully. Of course, imagining non-Western populations as necessarily following a Western path is itself open to debate, but the demographic literature tends to assume it.

On the margins of Europe we find a wide range of characteristics. Demographic aging came comparatively late in Russia, but the state and some businesses made modest contributions to the support of the aged. Imperial Russia, for example, offered some pensions to government employees, but in the late 1890s, "slightly more than 1 percent of the elderly population of the Empire lived on income from their capital and property, and another small group of mostly old women lived on remittances from relatives. Less than 1 percent of the elderly population received pensions" (Lindenmeyr, p. 236). Employees of railroads and some private enterprises experienced the beginning of pension programs, but any widespread benefits awaited the Soviet period. There would be a significant increase in the percentage receiving public pensions as the Soviet state evolved, but the end of the Soviet Union meant yet another shift in the history of the aged. The predominant pattern in pre-Revolutionary Russia was to work as long as possible or depend upon family or communal help. As Adele Lindenmeyr describes it, "A particularly common form of aid was '*po ocheredi*'; each household in the village provided food and shelter to a needy old man or woman in turn, while he or she moved from hut to hut, spending a day or week in each" (p. 238). Some almshouses existed, especially in towns, and some charities that served the aged were associated with the Orthodox Church. These were somewhat comparable to what was found in early modern western Europe. The diversity of the Russian Empire and the successor Soviet and post-Soviet Republics made for a wide range of experiences, from population structure to household structure.

Scholars looking back from the collapse of the Soviet bloc see important geographic differences. In 1990, 12.5% of the Czech population was 65 or over, as was 13.4% of the Hungarian population. In Bosnia-Herzegovina, it was only 6.5%, in Turkmenistan and Tajikistan less than 4%. The fertility decline in western Europe was paralleled by the phenomenon in parts of eastern Europe; thus, the population was comparably aged. Not so eastward to the Caucasus or central Asia. Muslim areas continued to have high fertility. Thus, the dependent population in European Russia tended to be old, while in central Asia it skewed young. Eastern Europe, however, experienced regression in life expectancy in the late 1960s and 1970s. Considerable progress came to several countries that gained independence in the post-Soviet era and joined the European Union. In Russia, by contrast, life expectancy took a turn for the worse. Causes of death varied in the former Soviet Union. Heart disease and stroke were dominant in the western part, with health deficits caused by smoking and alcoholism. In their later years, men were much more likely than women to be married. And women were more likely than men to live either alone or with children, thus being available to care for grandchildren (Velkoff and Kinsella).

The Japanese experience grew out of much quicker and later demographic aging than was found in Europe, and it resulted in unmatched aging. Yet Japanese cultural opposition to individualism meant maintenance of traditional living arrangements. Well into the contemporary era, rates of coresidence of the aged with their married or unmarried children were extremely high (Palmore). Eldest sons were privileged, and daughters-in-law had to adjust to powerful mothers-in-law. Indeed, there has been discussion of the unwillingness of Japanese women to marry first sons in recent times.

Historical experience mattered greatly, as the Second World War saw a greater economic role for women even as their eventual experience of old age in a traditional culture involved a narrowing of horizons. However, some changes were occurring on the eve of Japan's demographic aging. Scholars observed considerable matriarchal power in the home while patriarchal authority continued to hold sway in public (Freed, p. 244).

Japan headed the pack in East Asian economic development and demographic aging. South Korea, Taiwan, Hong Kong, and Singapore were next to industrialize, and all experienced falling fertility and mortality. Confucian ideas were harnessed in all of them to favor family over state support of the aged, but to one extent or another they increased the role of the state in the late twentieth and early twenty-first centuries. Singapore has emphasized most strongly the role of the family; its Central Provident Fund (CPF), founded in 1955, continues to be a mandatory savings scheme, but people have used some such funds for mortgage payments and the education of children, so the state is facing some challenges to play a bigger role (Angelique Chan, pp. 126–131). East Asian social security programs aimed particularly at the aged began at various points in the twentieth century (Japan in 1941, Taiwan in 1950, China and Malaysia in 1951, Singapore in 1953, Hong Kong in 1973, Korea in 1986, and Thailand in 1990), but a stronger state role came late in the century: Korea's National Pension scheme in 1988, Taiwan's National Health Insurance scheme in 1994 and National Pension Insurance in 2008, Hong Kong's Mandatory Provident Fund in 2000, and Japan's Long-Term Care Insurance in 2000. From 1990 to 2003, Japanese publicly funded cash benefits for the aged increased by a factor of 18, South Korea's by a factor of six (Fu and Hughes, pp. 2–3).

An extreme form of population aging can be found elsewhere in East Asia. China had been going through the usual elements of the demographic transition, but an extraordinary sort of aging has resulted from a single-minded policy of cutting fertility. Throughout the world, reduction in fertility resulted in population aging, but in China the process was accentuated by the one-child policy. Thus, a state-directed effort at reducing population has had an impact that might have been unintended but could easily have been predicted. Presumably, it was a matter of avoiding one demographic dilemma while bringing on another. Looking ahead from the early twenty-first century, Robert Stowe England writes that in China those aged 65 and older would go from seven percent of the population to between 25 and 30, 33 and 50 in some cities (England, p. xi.). Putting it another way, he argues that in half a century, China's elderly will outnumber the combined elders of North America, Europe, and Japan.

Unlike the more developed South Korea, Taiwan, Singapore, and Hong Kong, China would "become an aging country before it became a moderately developed country" (England, p. 1). Lin Jiang points out the combination of factors making for a very challenging situation: "the unprecedented pace of population aging, the size of the Chinese population, the country's lack of a social security system for the majority of its citizens, its low level of development, and the radical transformation of social and economic structures during the 1980s" (Lin Jiang, p. 423). Without significant social security in rural China, the policy of forced fertility decline would have serious repercussions for families that would traditionally be expected to care for the aged. The same policies that would yield demographic aging would put added pressure on smaller families. Yet Jiang's demographic simulations demonstrate that Chinese families would experience pressure from caring for the aged only during particular periods of the life course. And, as also became obvious in the West, increasing numbers of dependent elderly corresponded to declining numbers of dependent children. Jiang also pointed out that rural Chinese, understanding that having two children would eventually benefit them in old age, have resisted the one-child policy. The most serious problem, then, would arise for the childless aged, and it has been suggested that targeted social-security policies might deal effectively with that segment of the population.

Even in countries that did not reduce fertility as rapidly as Japan or in as draconian a fashion as China, reductions in morbidity and mortality led to increasing life expectancy and in growing numbers of aged people. Such is the case in significant parts of the global South. India's continued youthful population mitigated the aging of the total population, but Indians faced the challenges of modernity and post-modernity while holding on to traditional household structures. Adult sons had responsibility for aged parents, and on this score comparison can be made with Japan. But in the Indian case, the model was to continue to reside in the husband's parental home. Moreover, the declining mortality associated with modernity increased the chances of maintaining the supposedly traditional three-generation household. And, as Sylvia Vatuk points out, "the informal separation of elderly parents between the homes of different sons is a not uncommon solution to the problem of apportioning the responsibility for support among one's offspring – and perhaps incidentally to problems of marital incompatibility between elderly spouses" (Vatuk, p. 76). Vatuk also demonstrates an important urban/rural distinction, as young people left their villages for the city, while old people returned after urban careers (p. 95). At least that seemed to be the case in the 1980s, when she could write: "traditional cultural arrangements for old age security continue – even under rapidly changing social and economic conditions – to provide fairly adequately for the shelter and support needs of most aged Indians, within a family setting" (p. 97). More recent economic and cultural changes may have made that less plausible. Scholars who have examined Indian aging in an era of globalization find much to consider.

The Indian population aged 60 and above numbered 56 million in 1991 and 70 million in 1998; demographers at the turn of the century expected it to reach 177 million by 2025. But India is a diverse place, and a state like Kerala, characterized by much lower birthrates, greater literacy, and greater life expectancy, has a more "aged" profile than other regions. Kerala developed more than 30 different social security and welfare schemes for its aged, some fully funded by the state, others not. Elders in that state are aware of demographic progress, value whatever pensions they might receive (the percentage that does), and discuss possibilities of delaying retirement (for those who have the possibility). Like Indians in other states and territories, they greatly value intergenerational solidarity (Rajan, Mishra, and Sarna).

Anthropologist Sarah Lamb has examined aging in a rural Bengali village (*White Saris and Sweet Mangoes*). She refers to the Hindu ideas mentioned in chapter 3 but focuses on the networks people develop over the course of their lives and the perceived need to detach oneself in late life in preparation for death. The term for such social, bodily, and emotional networks is *maya*. She also speaks of recognized relations between generations across time and gendered differences in old age. She and medical anthropologist Lawrence Cohen have explored Indian gerontology's concern for the impact of modernization and urbanization on traditional arrangements. The most common theme in that literature is the breakup of the "joint family" and abandonment of the aged. It is said to take the form of a supposed tipping of authority from mothers-in-law to daughters-in-law. But she has also looked at the Indian diaspora in the US and its particular challenges of aging (*Aging and the Indian Diaspora*). Similarly, Katy Gardner has looked at a Bengali community in London (*Age, Narrative and Migration*). Her elders with roots in Bangladesh journey half-way around the world but also journey through the life course. "Home" is no longer in South Asia, nor is it exactly in London. Both places contribute to each person's narrative. Reading such works drives home the importance of economic change and international migration even as people carry in their heads ideas of cultural tradition. Transnational aging makes its way into an American physician's popular book on aging, with one chapter based on his correspondence with an Indian woman in her 70s with children in England and the United States (Nuland, *The Art of Aging*). She was looking for wisdom from an American doctor who had already written a book on death. As with Gardner's informants, wisdom would come out of the aging person's narrative.

In the late twentieth and early twenty-first centuries, African populations still had lower life expectancies than people elsewhere, but much of that had to do with diseases of the young, whether infants from disease that had not been controlled by public health measures or young adults who were affected by the AIDS epidemic. This meant that elders, who had traditionally exercised considerable authority when holding onto resources, had important roles to play, especially in rural areas. A study of intergenerational relations in Ghana demonstrates some new tensions but also traditional hierarchies. Isabella Aboderin's *Intergenerational Support and Old Age in Africa* speaks of a "contract" of familial duties. "Rather than being negotiated however, this contract was imposed by the divine and natural order of life, and made parents the more powerful party – as they enjoyed an unconditional entitlement to support" (Aboderin, p. 100). But she finds a shift in normative attitudes and expectations in the recent past (p. 137). What had been unconditional intergenerational support was becoming conditional. The key change has been urbanization, and middle generations found themselves focusing more on themselves and their children than on the aged (p. 146). Even more particularly, old men were finding themselves at a disadvantage, presumably because families had a more vivid memory of the roles older women had played earlier in the history of their households (pp. 152–156). Pension systems were looking increasingly necessary. But except for South Africa, Botswana, and Namibia, sub-Saharan Africa had little in the way of pensions.

Those pensions that did exist were to be had primarily in cities, where certain kinds of work, particularly in the public sector, predominated. But in the African countryside (like rural areas of Asia) there were almost no such arrangements.

Moreover, the high rates of rural-to-urban migration by younger people left many elders to their own devices. How this worked out has varied by time and place. Scholars such as Megan Vaughan and James Ferguson have investigated the history of migration in Zambia (including in its earlier form as Northern Rhodesia). They called into question the idea that there was any simple evolution from a period of circular migration (between country and city) to one of temporary urbanization and then more permanent settlement in the city. They found a variety of practices that often depended upon economic circumstances. Men who migrated to work in the Copperbelt went elsewhere in periods of economic downturn. Some returned to the country; others moved from city to city. But eventually a great many sought to move to a home region, not necessarily a home village. Such retirement often came after years of visits and periodic delivery of remittances by which people invested in kin.

In the best of circumstances, rural areas provided opportunities for what was perceived to be a good old age, but sometimes the urban experience changed people's ideas and comportment, and rural kin and neighbors did not always approve of such change. Recent scholarship has revealed intergenerational tensions that are thought to be unprecedented. One study of disadvantaged South African elders yields complaints that younger generations not only ignore and sometimes abuse them but that they have little appreciation for what they had gone through in the colonial and Apartheid eras. Personal loss and sorrow were combined with a loss of historical memory.

Epidemic disease has compounded difficulties. Consider what happened when the HIV/AIDS crisis hit Uganda. Grandparents found themselves increasingly caring for orphaned grandchildren, with no adult children available to support them. Alun Williams, in *Ageing and Poverty in Africa: Ugandan Livelihoods in a Time of HIV/AIDS,* offers a portrait of a poor rural community.

> The AIDS epidemic's influence on older people's lives is multi-faceted. Firstly, as sexually active adults, they are vulnerable to infection. Second, as parents, they are required to provide the physical, emotional, and economic resources necessary to care for, and later bury, their children who have AIDS. Thirdly, as grandparents, they are similarly required to care for orphans, to feed, clothe and educate them, and care for them if they are sick. Finally, as dependent old people, they are deprived of any support in their old age that their adult children might have provided. Whilst each of these brings its own difficulties, it is quite possible that two, three, or all four of these eventualities will happen, simultaneously, to the same aged individual.
>
> (p. 196)

Williams draws attention to the way long-term rural-to-urban migration patterns among young adults and deep-rooted cultural norms surrounding kinship roles put grandparents into caregiving roles of enormous responsibility. They worried about their ability to fulfill such roles even as they dealt with grief, sadness, and loss.

In North Africa, research on the roles of older men and women reveals different patterns from place to place. In Egypt, aged women have exercised less authority than aged men, but home ownership and widowhood improved their positions. By contrast, in Tunisia a more "gender equitable" situation obtained. In such circumstances, widowhood did not bring greater power (Yount and Agree). Such regional and cultural differences indicate the difficulty of generalizing. Nonetheless, some commonalities are found across the "developing" world. The peak period for family authority in Korea, Singapore, the Philippines, Taiwan, and Egypt has been the early stage of later life. Then, with cognitive and physical decline, authority also declines (Yount and Agree, p. 127). In some ways we're back at the anthropological approach and the ideas associated with modernization. But the pace of change has often quickened, and we have better data than for the past in the global South.

Economists looking for a region that might negotiate the last part of the demographic transition, population aging, in a way that avoided some of the problems of Europe, North America, and Japan looked to Latin America. There, fertility was only beginning to decline in much of the continent, and life expectancy went up. Thus, eventual aging could be predicted, but the challenges might be mitigated by the presence of many people of working age. Economists describe this as a "demographic bonus." In other words, as Latin America moved towards an "aged" population structure, it did not have the kind of dependency ratios (dependents per active worker) that were challenging other regions. It was thought that they would have a window of opportunity to anticipate the most difficult aspects of demographic aging.

Consider the experience of Brazil. Mortality fell significantly across the second half of the twentieth century, with infant mortality decreasing from 135 to 20 per thousand live births and life expectancy at birth going from 50.9 years in the early 1950s to 72.3 years in 2005–2010. That placed Brazil between Europe and East Asia. Brazil's increase from 50 to 70 years took 50 years. Western Europe took longer, but Japan (27 years) and Korea (33 years) were quicker. Even more dramatic than Brazil's decline in mortality was its fall in fertility. While it took European countries half a century to a century to reduce total fertility rates (TFR) to 2, it took Brazil a mere 17.5 years to go from 3 to 2 (Gragnolati, Jorgensen, Rocha, and Fruttero, pp. 45–51). Demographers note that, as of 2011, Argentina, Chile, and Uruguay had a higher percentage of elderly than Brazil, whose relative youth might translate into a temporary advantage. Still, it was projected that by mid-century, Brazil would have a higher proportion of aged than Europe did in 2010 (pp. 60–62). Another useful measure of the temporary advantage came in the form of dependency ratios, which went down with declining fertility but were projected to start up again because of demographic aging by 2020. Of course, the nature of that dependency will have shifted from the needs of children and educational institutions to the needs of the elderly and health care. Economists working under the auspices of the World Bank evaluated turn-of-the-century pension reforms, economic behavior across the life course, and particularly savings, and they urged the country to take advantage of the "demographic bonus."

Demographers, economists, and a variety of non-governmental organizations have all issued warnings of demographic aging to come. Sometimes the tone is shrill. However, much like development economists of the 1950s and 1960s, who wrote about lessons drawn from European industrialization, they anticipate opportunities for non-Western societies to recapitulate Western experience in a more self-conscious way. They're not necessarily fully aware of the implications of making the West the norm for everyone else. As in addressing other global themes such as human rights and environmental protection, experts offered lessons from the West and pleas to avoid its "mistakes." The pattern is one of seeing the world as more interdependent and learning from one another's experiences. The theme of "lessons learned" is one that puts scientific experts in a position to encourage particular sorts of policies. In the final two chapters, we will examine the emergence of international fields of geriatrics and gerontology and their ways of understanding current and anticipated experiences of aging.

Works Cited and Further Reading

Adele Lindenmeyr, "Work, Charity, and the Elderly in Late-Nineteenth-Century Russia," in *Old Age in Preindustrial Society*, edited by Peter N. Stearns (NY: Holmes and Meier, 1982); Victoria A. Velkoff and Kevin Kinsella, *Aging in Eastern Europe and the Former Soviet Union* (US Department of Commerce, Bureau of the Census, 1993).

Erdman Palmore, *The Honorable Elders: A Cross-Cultural Analysis of Aging in Japan* (Durham, NC: Duke University Press, 1975); Anne O. Freed, *The Changing Worlds of Older Women in Japan* (Manchester, CT: Knowledge, Ideas, and Trends, 1992); Angelique Chan, "Ageing in Singapore: Policy Challenges and Innovations," in Tsung-hsi Fu and Rhidian Hughes, eds., *Ageing in East Asia: Challenges and Policies for the Twenty-First Century* (London and NY: Routledge, 2009); Robert Stowe England, *Aging China: The Demographic Challenge to China's Economic Prospects*, The Washington Papers/182, Published with the Center for Strategic and International Studies, Washington, DC (Westport, CT: Praeger, 2005); Lin Jiang, "Parity and Security: A Simulation Study of Old-age Support in Rural China," *Population and Development Review*, Vol. 20, No. 2 (June 1994): 423–448.

Sylvia Vatuk, "Old Age in India," in Stearns, *Old Age in Preindustrial Society*; S. Irudaya Rajan, U.S. Mishra, and P. Sankara Sarna, *India's Elderly: Burden or Challenge?* (New Delhi, Thousand Oaks, London: Sage, 1999); Sarah Lamb, *White Saris and Sweet Mangoes: Aging, Gender and Body in North India* (Berkeley: University of California Press, 2000), and *Aging and the Indian Diaspora: Cosmopolitan Families in India and Abroad* (Bloomington: Indiana University Press, 2009); Katy Gardner,

Age, Narrative and Migration: The Life Course and Life Histories of Bengali Elders in London (Oxford: Berg, 2002); Lawrence Cohen, *No Aging in India: Alzheimer's, the Bad Family, and Other Modern Things* (Berkeley: University of California Press, 1998); Sherwin B. Nuland, *The Art of Aging: A Doctor's Prescription for Well-Being*, chapter 6 (NY: Random House, 2007).

Isabella Aboderin, *Intergenerational Support and Old Age in Africa* (New Brunswick and London: Transaction Publishers, 2006); Henrietta L. Moore and Megan Vaughan, *Cutting Down Trees: Gender, Nutrition, and Agricultural Change in the Northern Province of Zambia, 1890–1990* (Portsmouth, NH: Heinemann, 1994); James Ferguson, *Expectations of Modernity: Myths and Meanings of Urban Life on the Zambian Copperbelt* (Berkeley: University of California Press, 1999). On elders' ideas about dying and the good death, see Sjaak Van Der Geest, "'I Want to Go!' How Older People in Ghana Look Forward to Death," *Ageing & Society* 22 (2002): 7–28. On intergenerational conflict, see Els Van Dongen, "Remembering in Times of Misery: Can Older People in South Africa 'Get Through'?" *Ageing and Society* 25 (2005): 525–541. On epidemic disease, see Alun Williams, *Ageing and Poverty in Africa: Ugandan Livelihoods in a Time of HIV/AIDS* (Aldershot: Ashgate, 2003). On aging and gender in North Africa, see Kathryn M. Yount and Emily M. Agree, "The Power of Older Women and Men in Egyptian and Tunisian Families," *Journal of Marriage and Family*, Vol. 66, No. 1 (Feb. 2004): 126–146.

Michele Gragnolati, Ole Hagen Jorgensen, Romera Rocha, Anna Fruttero, *Growing Old in Older Brazil: Implications of Population Aging on Growth, Poverty, Public Finance, and Service Delivery* (Washington, DC: The World Bank, 2011).

12

AGING, MEDICALIZATION, AND THE DISCIPLINE OF GERONTOLOGY

Medical attention to aging is hardly a new phenomenon. In cultures East and West, traditional ways of dealing with the infirmities of advanced age are well known. The existence of such literature has made it clear that dealing with individual aging has almost always had a scientific or medical component. Natural remedies, supposedly healthful diets, and recommendations of moderation in all things are legion. Yet it is fair to say that in the modern period there has been greater attention given to clinical treatment of diseases of the aged, and in the natural, behavioral, and social sciences specialization in the plight of the elderly has become increasingly common. Thus, we see the emergence of medical institutions for the aged as well as a social scientific discipline of gerontology. Geriatrics and gerontology display their medical and scientific origins in emphasizing pathology and social problems, but they have been known to employ a more optimistic language of adaptive, normal, and healthy aging.

Historians of medicine rely on limited evidence to describe how the ailments associated with old age were represented in such places as Meso-America, India, China, Mesopotamia, and Egypt. The Incas seemed to distinguish among older people who still walk well, those who have no teeth and limited hearing, those who do nothing other than eat and sleep, and those even older. Peruvian medical treatments included purges and bleedings; pre-Columbian sculpture included wrinkled, toothless, and feeble aged characters. The Aztecs had words referring to old people and reserved maize beer for elders, but dying of old age appears to have been less glorious than dying at a time of strength. Ancient Babylonian texts refer to treating white hair and give voice to the ailing old: "I am forgotten..., my strength has disappeared, the wine that revivifies men no longer has any effect on me" (Martin, p. 46).

Egyptian texts are among the oldest that can be called geriatric. As we saw in chapter 3, they speak of an ideal life course as lasting 110 years and include preventive measures, clinical observations, and therapeutic recommendations. The vizir Imhotep supposedly had remedies for the ailments of advanced age, and the aging process itself was described as a weakening of the circulation of blood and of respiration. Several papyri mention the experience of memory loss, rheumatism, trembling, white hair, and wrinkles as well as remedies made from fig, celery, honey, and other products.

It's possible to find descriptions of ailments of the aging body and recommendations for herbal treatments in both China and India. Until the production of the *Manual of Internal Medicine of the Yellow Emperor*, compiled in the Han dynasty (200 BC to 200 AD), the Chinese seemed to limit themselves to philosophical reflections. Yet that philosophical background provided (and still provides) an alternative to Western models. "Nourishing life" involved preservation of vital energy rather than treating disease. Ideally, one cares for oneself before developing symptoms and requiring intervention. However, when a malady emerged out of disequilibrium of yin and yang, appropriate remedies were identified. The pharmacopeia of the legendary emperor Shen Nong (Divine Farmer) listed 347 vegetable, animal, and mineral products, and the Daoist alchemist and theologian Tao Hongjing (456–536 CE) added another 365 substances. In India, the *Sushruta Samhita* described health as coming from the harmony of elementary substances of the body and suggested that life was preprogrammed to go through periods of growth, aging, and death. Ayurvedic medicine proposed certain herbs, most notably ambrosia, to delay the process.

In the West, as we have already seen, Hippocrates and Galen stand as the most important physicians of the ancient world. Hippocratic texts describe the role of humors but also observe how some maladies manifested themselves differently at different ages. Galen provided a link from Greece to Rome and, in a seeming echo of the Indian *Sushruta Samhita*, spoke of how every living creature has in itself from the beginning the germ of its own death. Western medicine relied on Hippocrates and Galen for centuries. In the Christian Middle Ages, illness was associated more with sin, but physicians in the Arabic-speaking world, including Jews, Christians, and Muslims, preserved ancient learning and displayed an openness to other ideas. Avicenna wrote on cerebral function, and Arab medicine more generally, in describing natural, non-natural, and extra-natural phenomena, approached aging as a natural process. Arab and Jewish texts explored aging and memory and associated old age with wisdom.

In the Renaissance, it is possible to speak of an anatomical revolution with Leonardo Da Vinci, and early modern medicine (André du Laurens, Francis Bacon, René Descartes, Georg Ernst Stahl, Georges-Louis Leclerc, comte de Buffon) describes aging in scientific language. Yet, even into the eighteenth century, traditional wisdom held an important place. Herman Boerhaave (1668–1738), a noted Dutch doctor and chemist, publicized the method, mentioned in antiquity, of having an elderly man sleep between two young women; there was no comparable recommendation for an elderly woman. Doctors recommended transfusions, magnetism, a celestial bed that combined electricity, scent, and sound, etc. Much of this strikes us as fanciful; yet, progress was being made in anatomy and in the organization of the medical world.

Contemporary geriatricians tend to trace their roots back to practitioners and authors in the second half of the nineteenth century, when clinical medicine offered close study of the aging subject, and the early twentieth century, when the fields of "geriatrics" and "gerontology" were both named. The second half of the nineteenth century would see a shift from a preventive way of thinking to a more curative one, with some disease in old age no longer accepted as completely unavoidable. But we would be remiss to ignore the increasing specialization in medical publication in the eighteenth century and the emergence of clinical medicine in Paris in the first half of the nineteenth. The turbulence of the French Revolutionary period opened a space for the emergence of large hospitals, with a focus on medical care and research. Some of the literature speaks of progress in Paris until 1848; Michel Foucault emphasizes the disciplinary and controlling aspects of clinical medicine; Jean-Pierre Martin sees the first half of the nineteenth century as preparing the way for great advances in the second half of the century. He cites the work of Pinel on dementia (1801) and Esquirol on paralysis, Benjamin Rush on the diseases of the aged in Philadelphia, and Léon Rostan on asthma and aging (1830). Prus' 1840 treatise on diseases of the aged was a systematic work of necropsy, with examination of the organs of 390 old people between the ages of 60 and 90. Cruveilhier's atlas of pathological anatomy explored senile pathology. Other doctors throughout Europe examined aging by focusing on circulation, respiration, digestion, sexual function, the senses, sleep, memory, and judgment. But the real turning point is often identified with the *Leçons cliniques sur les maladies des vieillards* of Jean-Martin Charcot, published first in 1866 and in augmented editions down to 1890. It was the first such study to include precise medical drawings of the organs of aged individuals.

Archival study of hundreds of observations by Charcot of aged patients in the Salpêtrière, the Paris hospital that served large numbers of poor, aged women, reveals clinical histories, autopsies, charts of temperature and pulse, and illustrations of lesions. Charcot summarized much of what happened to the aging body as "atrophy," but he also found that if some bodily functions were growing weaker, some organs acquitted themselves as well as in earlier adulthood. So he classified diseases of the aged into three groups: those that were peculiar to the aged, those that display a particular character in advanced age, and those that were rare in old age. Medical historian Alain Lellouch locates Charcot's advance as a moment of transition from a medicine of the hospital to a medicine of the laboratory. Charcot built on his predecessors' work on hospital populations, but he anticipated something that would develop later in more impressive fashion in Germany, the adoption of laboratory methods to care for hospital patients. Lellouch explains the importance of Paris in this transition by pointing to three phenomena: the beginnings of an aging of the French population, particularly in certain regions, the concentration of old subjects in large hospitals, and the role played by physicians interested in clinical anatomy. Charcot and his colleagues had a place to observe patients and to inspect cadavers. Later in his career, Charcot would turn to the study of hysteria and psychology. Freud would observe his work. But what made his career and represented a founding moment for what would later be named geriatrics was his work on the aged. This is not to say that most elderly people saw doctors regularly. Peter Stearns has made that point. But it is possible to see a genealogy of geriatricians from then on. One of the keys to Charcot's success was his openness to international developments, particularly in England and Germany. From then on, his own work would be seen as foundational in an international field. His book was published in the United States in 1881 and drew considerable attention.

The "heroic" story of Parisian geriatric medicine must be understood as contemporary with continued use of medicinal plants, important developments in hygiene and public health, the increasing popularity of thermal cures (taking the waters) in both the metropole and the Empire, and early research efforts in endocrinology. Among the French physicians who joined endocrinology to the medical study of old age were Claude Bernard and his student, Charles-Édouard Brown-Séquard, who injected himself and many others seeking to stem the aging process with extracts of bull testicles. Brown-Séquard directed the prestigious laboratory of the Collège de France, which produced enough extract for 200,000 injections. Other practitioners tried other animals, from guinea pigs and sheep to dogs and monkeys. They even referred to such practices as "*séquardothérapie.*"

Such ideas traveled widely, as did ideas of the degeneration of tissue and devolution of cells. For geriatrics, one of the important routes was from Europe to the United States, and it was the Viennese-born American physician I.L. Nascher who named the field in a 1909 article and his 1914 book: *Geriatrics: The Diseases of Old Age and their Treatment*. Carole Haber, who has written about the founding of American geriatrics, refers to Nascher's difficulty in distinguishing between normal and diseased states of the elderly and the tendency among physicians to represent old age as a pathological state. Nascher had named a new specialty, but there were as yet few volunteers to take it up.

Still, research continued, and ideas spread. Early in the twentieth century Ferran linked aging to a weakening of the nervous system and a rejection of waste materials by cells and organisms. Élie Metchnikoff, who first used the term "gerontology" at the Pasteur Institute in 1903, thought that aging came from general atrophy, disequilibrium between cells, and a poisoning from toxins in the intestines. For him, phagocytes that had normally protected tissue turned against tissues in the senescent body. He recommended good intestinal microbes, which might come from the eating of sour milk or yogurt. Medical historian Jean-Pierre Martin points out that the author of one treatise on maladies of old people, Rauzier, wanted to substitute maladies *in* old people for the term maladies *of* old people to make the point that one could be old but not senile and vice versa. But most important from a medical point of view in the early twentieth century was improvement in microscopy and pathology.

A very important development in pathology as applied to mental health came from Aloïs Alzheimer, who described presenile dementia in 1906. Emil Kraeplin used the term "Alzheimer's Disease" in 1910. Further advances came much later in the century—we will address the topic of Alzheimer's disease and its cultural importance in the next chapter—but vaccines and cures remain elusive. Meanwhile, doctors studied atherosclerosis and spoke of vascular, nutritive, and self-poisoning theories of aging. One could find attempts to study aging as related to circulation, respiration, digestion, the nervous system, urination, the skin, and almost anything else. Research into geriatric medicine was becoming more common even if doctors wouldn't have defined themselves as having a geriatric specialty.

In the post-Second World War period, important changes in geriatrics were linked to the major discoveries in medicine generally. For example, antibiotics helped patients of all ages but were particularly important for the aged. Changes in medical technology were important as well. Hormone therapy and cellular therapies were of note, and plastic surgery had applications for the aging. Cataract surgery, organ transplant, and the invention of artificial organs made a big difference. Even more important was medical attention throughout the life course, beginning in childhood. Social policies that provided healthcare had an impact on survival into late life. In the last decades of the twentieth century, researchers paid attention to cardiovascular disease, Parkinson's, Alzheimer's, and gene therapies. Theories proliferated concerning molecular and cellular health. It would be difficult to list everything of note. But we should make clear that important developments occurred at both micro and macro levels. Challenges came from the very small, the failure of cells to replicate, and the very large, the difficulty of covering everyone in a population. But at both ends, the medical or scientific model was key.

In the early twentieth century, geriatrics and gerontology shared common roots. As Stephen Katz points out, medicine and science played essential roles in the formation of a discipline called gerontology. But while geriatrics and gerontology developed on similar tracks, geriatrics would remain a medical term while gerontology in the mid-twentieth century came to be a multidisciplinary enterprise, extending to virtually all the social sciences and occasionally the humanities. Yet, gerontology's scientific origins, including social scientific ones, are important to appreciate if we are to understand its subsequent development. Just as the patients in the Salpêtrière were important to Charcot's innovations in the medial care of the aged, so the inmates of almshouses, who tended to be elderly, provided subjects for thinking about old age. As we saw in the chapter on pensions, almshouses drew considerable attention, as Western publics engaged in debates over poverty, work, retirement, and the aging body. Private and public pensions were on the agenda throughout the Western world, and demographers were beginning to pay attention to aging. Many of the most influential demographers expressed alarm at declining birthrates and in their individual national contexts presented population aging as a sign of economic and moral degeneration. Social scientists undertook social surveys to address the problems of the aged, and the ingredients of a new discipline came together. Charles Booth and B. Seebohm Rowntree in England, Herbert Brown Ames in Canada, and I.M. Rubinow in the United States all contributed to a genre in which the aged were defined by their problems.

Some authors reached wide readerships with their views of the aged. In 1905, the Canadian physician William Osler, a distinguished faculty member at the Johns Hopkins University in Baltimore, gave a lecture he entitled "The Fixed Period." He had borrowed the title from a story by the English novelist Anthony Trollope and spoke of the creative period of life as running from age 25 to 40. He recommended rest after 60. Trollope's story called for the chloroforming of people at age 67½, and scandalized listeners took Osler as favoring such a policy. Osler, who was quite active long past the so-called creative period, had spoken playfully, but the press took him more seriously, and the idea of the "fixed period" became widely used. More positive views of old age emerged in the social sciences. G. Stanley Hall, a key figure in the professionalization of psychology in the United States, having published a widely read book called *Adolescence* in 1904, produced *Senescence* in 1922. To be sure, Hall looked to medicine, biology, and psychology, but he insisted on the importance of the humanities for understanding the process of aging, something gerontologists would not take up seriously for decades.

Social science, as applied to aging, had an important prehistory as well. In its early days in the Enlightenment, we find practitioners of what would become demography, and in the work of Condorcet we find someone who contemplated extending the life course indefinitely. With the Belgian statistician Adolphe Quetelet we find the idea of the "average man" and, consequently, average life expectancy. In Europe in the first half of the nineteenth century and in the United States in the second, we find numerous applications of mathematics to social questions. Social surveys, initially focused on matters of poverty and public health, began to study the elderly in particular. Historians of the turn-of-the century pension movement have described how the creators and purveyors of those surveys contributed to an image of the aged as poor and dependent. An entire population of people was being defined as a problem, carved out of a larger collective body.

Although it would be fair to say that the medical profession and the social sciences were defining the aged as needy, it was the identification of older people as a group that also allowed older people to act collectively, sometimes organizing themselves as interest groups in electoral politics. Thus, they pushed for pensions and social security in the first half of the twentieth century and came to play a powerful role in some countries in the second half. Yet, for much of the twentieth century, it was the tendency to understand the aged as a needy group that was most influential.

By the post-Second World War period, gerontology and geriatrics were associated with professional journals and even some that reached beyond professionals to a broader reading public. The journals often grew out of professional associations, and both provided a certain intellectual capital. The American Geriatrics Society was founded in 1942, the Gerontological Society in 1945. The latter became the Gerontological Society of America in 1980. The *Journal of Gerontology* began publication in 1946, and a wider-ranging journal called *The Gerontologist* began appearing in 1961. The Spanish Society of Geriatrics and Gerontology dates to 1948, the Italian Society of Geriatrics to 1949, and the French Society of Geriatrics and Gerontology to 1960. The British Geriatrics Society was founded in 1959, with the first British chair in geriatrics being created in Glasgow in 1965. The Danish Society of Geriatrics was founded in 1972.

Professional societies, publications, and eventually pharmaceutical companies did much to expand the reach of Western geriatrics and gerontology to the wider world, which tried to steer between indigenous wisdom and the more cosmopolitan, professional sort. As we move to the present, we witness the emergence of an international literature in gerontology that relies upon Western-style expertise to take account of aging around the world. Even as the literature comes to be produced in non-Western countries and sometimes attempts to bring to bear local knowledge, it also laments how "behind" the not-yet-aged countries are. For example, a recent study of Korean aging almost apologizes for the fact that as late as 1995 there had been very little activity by Korean sociologists in gerontology (Ahn Kye Choon and Chung Kyung Hee, p. 40). It expressed a desire to catch up and represented a mediated encounter between the professional gaze and local ways of being.

Yet, the focus on demographic aging and the related spread of gerontological knowledge may draw too much attention away from more local histories. Until very recently, the literature on Indian aging looked essentially at old cultural traditions and very contemporary social developments. Now a study on old age in the period from 1940 to 1960 gives hints of a different chronology. Kavita Sivaramakrishnan identifies two important connections with the West: the British Beveridge Plan that had an offshoot in India in the work of a committee headed by B.P. Adarkar, the "little Beveridge," that produced a report on social insurance and the arrival in India of American-trained social workers. But there was already an Indian context for what came to be considered the problems of the aged. It of course included the challenge posed by urbanization to the "joint family," but it also was greatly influenced by issues of labor and the family, anxiety surrounding new nationhood, and the pressure of Partition and mass migration. Indian old age became its own kind of "problem" that preceded any demographic aging and was not linked to an age group *per se*. This might not be so surprising when one considers that in the West old age emerged as a social "problem" before the dramatic aging of its populations, but it does complicate a world history consisting of multiple strands.

One of the most important characteristics of gerontology, as identified by gerontologists themselves, is its multidisciplinarity. The field of gerontology encompasses all of the social sciences as well as practitioners of the health sciences and humanities. As Thomas Cole, Stephen Katz, and others pointed out in the 1980s and 1990s, one way in which it tries to present a coherent front is through the publication of handbooks and multi-authored essay collections, whether to give an overview of gerontology as a whole or to define the key issues in particular branches of the field. Multiple editions of handbooks of aging and the social sciences as well as aging and the humanities provide useful surveys of a wide range of gerontological matters. Such publications show no signs of abating. A look at a few of the most recent can provide a good sense of current trends in gerontology.

Two gerontologists who have had long and distinguished careers in the United States, Vern L. Bengston and K. Warner Schaie, have edited a *Handbook of Theories of Aging*. After a section that explores theory-building in itself, as it relates to aging, we find sections devoted to biological and biomedical concepts and theories, psychological ones, and social scientific ones. The biological and biomedical contributions discuss genetics, evolution, neuropsychological theories of stress, health, and age-dependent diseases; the psychological concepts and theories touch upon ideas of a "fourth age" (the old old), competence, cognition, personality change and continuity, self-concepts, and emotions. The social scientific section explores anthropological and ethnographic models, social constructivist investigations, life course perspectives, social-structural models, and political economy theories of aging. In the spirit of a handbook, it includes a section on applications to public policy and encouraging a "good old age."

A more recent overview organized by scholars based in Germany and Great Britain, but published in the United States, is Hans-Werner Wahl, Clemens Tesch-Römer, and Andreas Hoff, eds., *New Dynamics in Old Age: Individual, Environmental, and Societal Perspectives*. The book covers contemporary gerontology by exploring five environments that it calls social, home, outdoor, technological, and societal. Some contributions are more explicit than others in calling for a global reach and cross-cultural sensitivities and some are focused on the peculiarities of wealthy societies, but in general their terms can be deployed internationally: social construction of age; physical and mental function; cohort differences; family relations; autonomy in a context of frailty; housing; relocation trauma; urban deprivation; outdoor mobility; driving and quality of life; leisure; the internet and technology in the home; labor and consumption markets. Like fellow gerontologists around the world, they explore employment and retirement, the fragility and chronic diseases that come with the "fourth age," the scientific management of old age, politics and policy, and differences among generational and cohort effects as people age.

A British handbook, *The Cambridge Handbook of Age and Ageing*, offers a similar, and similarly useful, overview of theory, the aging body, the aging mind, the aging self, the aging of relationships, the aging of societies, and policies and provisions for older people. Particular topics include biodemography and epidemiology, sensory impairment, mobility, psychological approaches, memory, intelligence, and wisdom, everyday competence, emotion, personality, depression, and dementia, self and identity, stress, reminiscence, religion, death, global aging and families, intergenerational relationships, grandparenthood, caregiving, gay and lesbian elders, life course perspectives, gender and inequality, feminist perspectives, work and retirement, ethical dilemmas in caring for the aged, nursing, managed care, and new technologies. Aging seems to be about everything.

Even handbooks that claim to narrow the focus take on an extraordinary array of topics. *The Sage Handbook of Social Gerontology*, edited by Dale Dannefer and Chris Phillipson, includes chapters written by gerontologists from four continents and, far from limiting itself to sociological perspectives, casts a wide net to include epidemiology and economics, health, religion, and stress, migration, care, and ethics. To point out the wide range is not to criticize. Gerontology is seemingly about everything. A very recent French survey of sociological views of old age and aging, *Vieillesses et vieillissements: Regards sociologiques*, edited by Cornelia Hummel, Isabelle Mallon, and Vincent Caradec, casts an almost equally wide net. But rather than begin with theory and demography, it begins with the political construction of old age as a problem. It explores social policies having to do with norms, retirement, intergenerational equity, dependence, long-term care, and Alzheimer's disease. It moves on to the diversity of experiences and perspectives, from feminism, migration, and national policy differences to social participation, grandparenthood, senior life, residential mobility, and retirement. A last section on the experience of aging for the self and the other deals with transitions in old age, food and domestic organization, sociability and solitude, living in institutions, caring for aged parents, legal protections, and caring for dependent elders.

It almost doesn't matter where the research is being done. The models are international. An Argentinian study of sexuality and aging collects local data and deploys a theoretical literature from Switzerland, France, and the United States (Gastron, Oddone, and Lynch). Scholarly frameworks are globalized, and often the terms of debate have their origins in the West. The menu of theories provided in the *Cambridge Handbook of Age and Ageing* makes that clear. Biomedical theories that range from "insults" from the environment to genetic disorders and cellular aging, psychological theories of lifespan development, cognition, or personality, and sociological and cultural theories that range from disengagement and age stratification to life course perspectives, feminism, and political economy all derive from Western scientific and academic thought and practice.

Sociological theories are most deeply embedded in the historical literature on old age and aging. It is possible to describe a first generation of sociological theory in the 1950s and 1960s as including disengagement, activity, and modernization. A second generation, from the 1970s and 1980s, includes theories of continuity, competence, exchange, age stratification, and political economy. The most popular theories in recent years have to do with life course, stratification, social construction, feminism, and political economy. The Cambridge authors also mention critical gerontology and postmodernism. Yet, a look at the literature on old age in past and present shows that even though professional discourses have changed, people who are writing about the autonomy of the aged, the mobility of generations, caregiving, and fragility in advanced age still find themselves falling back on revised ideas of disengagement/retreat, activity/autonomy, and what it means to be modern. Only "modern" now means multicultural and global, and the fourth age (old old) draws attention that used to focus on the third (young old), which Mary Catherine Bateson has named Adulthood II. We have arrived at the history of the present.

Works Cited and Further Reading

Jean-Pierre Martin, *La médecine des personnes âgées: de la préhistoire à nos jours* (Paris: L'Harmattan, 2012) – my translation of quotation; Jac. J. Janssen and Rosalind M. Janssen, *Getting Old in Ancient Egypt* (London: Rubicon, 1996); Erwin H. Ackerknecht, *Medicine at the Paris Hospital, 1794–1848* (Baltimore: Johns Hopkins University Press, 1967); Michel Foucault, *The Birth of the Clinic: An Archaeology of Medical Perception* (NY: Pantheon Books, 1973); Alain Lellouch, *Jean-Martin Charcot et les origines de la gériatrie: recherches historiques sur le fonds d'archives de la Salpêtrière* (Paris: Payot, 1993); Mark Micale, *Approaching Hysteria: Disease and its Interpretations* (Princeton: Princeton University Press, 1995); Peter N. Stearns, *Old Age in European Society: The Case of France* (NY: Holmes and Meier, 1976); Carole Haber, *Beyond Sixty-Five: The Dilemma of Old Age in America's Past* (NY: Cambridge University Press, 1983); Stephen Katz, *Disciplining Old Age: The Formation of Gerontological Knowledge* (Charlottesville: University of Virginia Press, 1996); W. Andrew Achenbaum, *Crossing Frontiers: Gerontology Emerges as a Science* (Cambridge: Cambridge University Press, 1995).

Ahn Kye Choon and Chung Kyung Hee, "Ageing and Ageing Policies in the Republic of Korea," in Lee Hock Guan, ed., *Ageing in Southeast and East Asia: Family, Social Protection and Policy Changes* (Singapore: Institute of Southeast Asian Studies, 2008); Kavita Sivaramakrishnan, "Aging and Dependency in an Independent Indian Nation: Migrant Families, Workers and Social Experts (1940–60)," in *Journal of Social History*, Vol. 47, No. 4 (2014): 968–993; Lawrence Cohen, *No Aging in India: Alzheimer's, the Bad Family, and Other Modern Things* (Berkeley: University of California Press, 1998).

Thomas R. Cole, David D. Van Tassel, and Robert Kastenbaum, eds., *Handbook of the Humanities and Aging* (NY: Springer, 1992); Vern L. Bengston and K. Warner Schaie, eds., *Handbook of Theories of Aging* (NY: Springer, 1999); Hans-Werner Wahl, Clemens Tesch-Römer, and Andreas Hoff, eds., *New Dynamics in Old Age: Individual, Environmental, and Societal Perspectives* (Amityville: Baywood, 2007); M.L. Johnson, V.L. Bengston, P.G. Coleman, and T.B.L. Kirkwood, eds., *The Cambridge Handbook of Age and Ageing* (Cambridge: Cambridge University Press, 2006); Dale Dannefer and Chris Phillipson, eds., *The Sage Handbook of Social Gerontology* (London: Sage, 2010); Cornelia Hummel, Isabelle Mallon, and Vincent Caradec, eds., *Vieillesses et vieillissements: Regards sociologiques* (Rennes: Presses universitaires de Rennes, 2014); Liliana Gastron, Julieta Oddone, Gloria Lynch, "Les représentations sociales de la sexualité des femmes et des hommes dans la vieillesse et au cours de la vie: Les changements à travers le temps," in Monique Legrand and Ingrid Voléry, eds., *Genre et parcours de vie: vers une nouvelle police des corps et des âges?* (Nancy: Presses universitaires de Nancy, 2013), pp. 63–74; Mary Catherine Bateson, *Composing a Further Life: The Age of Active Wisdom* (NY: Knopf, 2010).

13

AGING IN PRESENT AND FUTURE

In the early twenty-first century, aging has become a topic of worldwide concern. In the West and some non-Western countries such as Japan, demographic aging has raised the specter of economic and political decline while spawning entire industries catering to the elderly. In the rest of the world, relatively high percentages of young people make demographic aging appear to be less of a challenge. Yet, even there increasing life expectancy means ever-increasing total numbers of elderly. Many of the same issues that arise in "age-transformed" populations obtain, ranging from medical coverage and housing to pensions and intergenerational relations.

To some extent, every culture relies upon its own wisdom (whether Cicero, Shakespeare, Confucius, Nursi, or Simone de Beauvoir), its own way of handling old age, its own social and cultural practices, its own household structures, its own ideas of community responsibility and individualism. But as populations around the world, through different paths, converge in facing older populations, we may find ways of recognizing the experience and dignity of others. One consequence, as already suggested in the last chapter, has been the development of an international specialists' way of thinking about aging. To describe aging and the aged in the present, we need to begin with that specialized knowledge. As scientific research exists on an international plane, with the transmission of ideas occurring with lightning speed, the current narrative may transcend certain sorts of differences. But before reaching such a conclusion, we should recognize a range of subdisciplines as well as the different experiences of subgroups.

Driving government and popular awareness of issues related to aging is the spread of demographic knowledge. A 2014 World Health Organization study indicates that one in seven persons in the world will be over the age of 60 in 2020. One in five will be over 60 in 2050, when that group will number two billion and outnumber children under five years old. We have already discussed how falling fertility was the driving force in demographic aging for most of the twentieth century. Demographers are now reporting on a different cause, aging from the top of the age pyramid. In other words, it's now often less about falling fertility and more about falling mortality.

Specialists understood this decades ago. An influential, week-long conference in Belgium in 1986 presented the challenge of population aging through a clever graphic symbol (*Populations âgées et révolution grise*). It showed a triangle superimposed upon a rectangle. It symbolized the shift from a triangular age pyramid that characterized populations in most places at most times—wide at the bottom representing large numbers of births and young people, narrow at the top—to an almost rectangular shape—a narrowing at the bottom and a broadening of the old at the top. The principal editor, Michel Loriaux, called for a "gray revolution," symbolizing the hair of the aging, the shadow of the newly shaped age pyramid/rectangle, and the wisdom of age. He dismissed a suggestion by a fellow demographer that people just have more children and pointed out that now aging is occurring from the top, as life expectancy at advanced age was growing. Among contributors to the volume were Peter Laslett, the British historian who was most vocal in calling for recognition of the novelty of the "third age" and "age-transformed" populations, and Joseph-Alfred Grinblat of the Population Division of the UN, who outlined a history by which the period 1950–1970 saw a world population getting younger while populations in the developed world were aging, the period 1970–1985 saw the world grow older everywhere but Africa, and the period 1985–2025 sees accelerated aging everywhere. It was already evident that China's population policy would lead to challenges for elders, not only from the simple change in fertility but also because of the cultural context of three-generation families, an economic context of financial flows from elders to adult children with fewer of those children per old person, and a political context of requiring Confucian support for the old. As had happened several times over the course of the twentieth century, the Chinese were expressing seemingly contradictory attitudes towards Confucian tradition. A 1980 marriage law, a 1982 constitution, and a 1985 inheritance law all spoke to children's obligations toward their aged parents. The Chinese government is still attempting to strengthen such obligations.

Demographers offered data not only of life expectancy at birth but also at older ages, and they debated whether it would make more sense to speak of life expectancy in good health, an idea that came from the US but was developed furthest in Canada. Just as they were speaking of the clustering of mortality in very advanced age, so they suggested a similar development in terms of sickness while the "rectangular curve" offered graphic representation of huge majorities living into old age. Thus, J.F. Fries published studies in the early 1980s on "compression of morbidity." This would have important implications because, if Fries was right, the aging of populations would not result in overwhelming healthcare costs, as years of ill health would cluster at the end. Such was one of the demographic models for developments in the rapidly aging Western world that were spread to the globe through an international scientific literature and the work of the United Nations. Data are now generated to compare global populations on the same basic scale.

Some scientists, hearkening back to a centuries-old literature on prolongevity, hold out hopes of infinite progress. Most are more measured in their estimates. But even if the maximum life expectancy remains around 120, as many believe it will, gerontologists recognize the significance of average expectancy approaching that maximum. They have asked themselves what would be the consequences if the entire world population or, at the very least, citizens of wealthy countries would live to 100. Gerontologist Mildred M. Seltzer makes that the premise of a book in which she asks various specialists to imagine the consequences for family, interpersonal relationships, individual development, public policy, and labor force participation and retirement. Along the way, they address matters of cognitive competence, political activity, duration of marriage and friendship, the likelihood of intergenerational conflict, the location of life's transitions, continuity of self, physical and mental frailty, financial pressures, the right to die, healthcare rationing, and the meaning of generation. Would great-grandchildren have responsibilities to great-grandparents? Or vice versa? And what about great-great-grandchildren? Would rates and timing of marriage and remarriage change dramatically? To put it another way, would one of the great accomplishments of humanity—a widely shared dramatic increase in life expectancy and guaranteed support in old age—be undone by social, economic, or political challenges?

One area that people fear will undergo enormous pressure as populations age is that of financing retirement pensions. We have already traced the history of the welfare state and its role in ensuring old age. Commentators in the late twentieth and early twenty-first centuries asked if the new norm of a healthy and reasonably secure retirement would last much longer. They pointed to an important paradox. In Europe in particular, people who were living unprecedentedly longer lives were also leaving the workforce at unusually early ages. Retirement, which in its early days corresponded to what people thought of as old age, was unlinked from late life. The "third age" now came to refer to a period of healthy leisure and consumption. At best, it meant an opportunity for adult education and personal development; yet, some observers associated it with a very traditional idea that had been linked to elder status: greed. They considered current systems unsustainable. Retirees would not be old for another 20 years. In France between 1975 and 2010 the expected period of retirement doubled from 10.6 to 20.4 years (Anne-Marie Guillemard, *Les défis du vieillissement*, p. 19). Median age of retirement in France had fallen to 58 years. In Europe the employment rate for those over 55 was only 35–39% (p. 24). If, as had been hoped by many, this had translated into jobs for younger people, it might have been acceptable. But it did not. To make matters worse, pensions were often underfunded. And in those countries characterized as "low-work" societies, people were using a variety of mechanisms for leaving the workforce. For example,

> In Austria, 75–80% of men who retired between 2000 and 2010 tried to do so by claiming an invalidity pension. More than half of them had their claims rejected, so less than half succeeded. Yet 71% of male farmers, for example, managed to retire as invalids in 2011, despite having longer-than-average life expectancy.
>
> *(Marin, p. 46)*

How odd to see a rise in disability claims in a population that is healthier and longer-lived. Could this be sustained? Or could societies figure out how to keep mature adults or, to use the term for those in the second half of their working lives, experienced but not yet old, "seniors" in the workplace?

In the most ambitious work on the future of pensions, Bernd Marin looked at the case of Austria, which he called a "low-work" or "idle society," in an international, comparative context. As a result of both demographic transition and the extraordinary achievements of the welfare state, Europeans needed to reinvent retirement by extending working life incentives. Marin pointed out that the challenge to stabilizing pensions came more from low employment rates than from demographic aging itself or risky financial markets. Pensions were "by far the most important single wealth entitlement in people's lives (around half a million US dollars on average in the OECD), exceeding many times over the private savings of the average individual and even of relatively well-off middle-class households" (p. 40). Some countries were beginning to find ways of keeping "seniors" in the labor market. Guillemard in France and Marin in Austria noted successes in Sweden, Finland, and Japan.

Marin points out a diversity of circumstances within and across societies. Thus, women's careers differed significantly from men's, and among women the patterns varied. He speaks of

> at least four different 'typical' female working-life courses: full-career women, women alternating between full-time and part-time work depending on their children's needs, women participating in the labour market for only ten years in the entire life course, and women working part-time for most of their career.
>
> *(p. 57)*

He points out extraordinary differences in life expectancy between long-lived Switzerland, Sweden, France, and Austria and short-lived Belarus and the Russian Federation. Most Russian men were dying before retirement age.

> While the probability today is that the majority of Austrian men will live beyond 80 years…, only one Russian man in eight ever survives that long. But once he survives to the age of 80, the chances are that he will reach 86 (rather than 88 for an Austrian of the same cohort).
>
> *(pp. 184–185)*

Russians were dying much earlier, but those who did reach old age would survive almost as long as their counterparts in Western Europe.

Individual countries were experimenting with adjustments to their pension systems. Australia, Italy, Poland, Slovakia, and Sweden created "defined-contribution" plans. Denmark "linked the legal pension age to changing life expectancy. France has extended the minimum contribution period (*cotisation*) required to qualify for a full entitlement because of developments in longevity. Finland and Portugal have made the benefits awarded automatically dependent on changing life expectancy" (p. 171). Marin recommends the Swedish "notional defined-contribution system" (NDC). This is a pay-as-you-go, defined-contribution system that is sensitive to changing workforce participation, with beneficiaries being paid from current workers' contributions in amounts their own contributions would have permitted. And those who want to receive more will have an incentive to work longer. Some countries provide generous unemployment benefits without doing much to reintegrate aging workers into the workforce; others provide less financial support for unemployment while encouraging adaptation to changing conditions; some leave people to the vagaries of the marketplace.

Studies such as those by Guillemard and Marin resist calls to privatize social security. They see possibilities of adapting the welfare state or "social state" to evolving circumstances. Like many others writing on such matters, they see the intergenerational contract that underlies pensions as worthy of preservation.

Debates about work and pensions often have at their root philosophical issues about intergenerational justice. Beginning in the 1980s and 1990s, some important publications were appearing—one involved historian Peter Laslett and political scientist James Fishkin (*Justice Between Age Groups and Generations*). The general public in the Anglophone world was introduced to such matters by Daniel Callahan, *Setting Limits: Medical Goals in an Aging Society*, with a particular focus on the financing and rationing of medical care. Philosophers paid more serious attention to the work of Norman Daniels, which coincided with debates in the United States on expanding medical coverage nationally (*Am I My Parents' Keeper?*). A small but noticeable movement had sprung up calling for a recalibration of responsibilities to obtain justice between young and old. Some voices accused elders of selfishness. Daniels called for a rethinking. He thought it unjust to pit young and old against one another. He observed that, unlike other forms of inequality, particularly between races and classes, inequality between generations could be ironed out if most people could expect to inhabit all the stages of life. We are all old, or will be. Thus, he talked about focusing upon entire lifetimes and financing what he called the "prudential lifespan account." Distinguished philosophers such as Bernard Williams and Ronald Dworkin contributed to the debate by questioning how long one would want to live and making suggestions about not providing life-extending treatment to dementing elderly. Jurist Richard Posner thought Dworkin's idea about withholding such treatment "beyond the gravitational field of American morality."

The philosophical literature took a turn in the early twenty-first century with Dennis McKerlie's 2001 article, "Justice Between the Young and the Old" and his 2012 book of the same name. McKerlie thought that Daniels' prudential lifespan approach ignored serious dilemmas when elders found themselves in serious difficulties and decreased autonomy. People do still have different life expectancies and different health histories. What does one do with people who would focus their resources on the period of adulthood and then find themselves dealing with serious health challenges in old age? Philosopher Angieszka Jaworska challenged Daniels on grounds that we should respect the views of those whose agency has been compromised. Alzheimer's patients, even having lost memory and a sense of continuity, still merit some degree of agency. One of the best guides to philosophical debates on aging is Helen Small's *The Long Life*, which greatly refines an approach made by Simone de Beauvoir. Beauvoir, while also surveying the social sciences, humanities and arts, had explored aged characters in literature to express her horror at aging. Small takes a more optimistic view and connects various philosophical approaches to a range of literary characters and themes as a way of addressing large philosophical issues. Thus, she uses Plato to read Thomas Mann, Aristotle to read Shakespeare, Derek Parfit to read Balzac, etc. Some aged characters come to us already old. Others evolve over the life course. Either way, they illustrate ongoing dilemmas of the aging self.

Philosophers who focus on intergenerational justice, as we have seen, have something to say to those who study pensions. They also have something to say to sociologists working on the changing nature of the life course, and philosophers who address questions of identity and of the evolving self share concerns with psychologists of aging. We turn now to the sociology and psychology of aging.

Sociologists have emphasized changes in the shape of the life course. When retirement was a relatively new phenomenon, it was common to see life as consisting of three stages: formation in youth, work in adulthood, and retirement in old age. That model, associated with the era of pension and welfare-state development, made it appropriate to theorize old age as a time of disengagement. But "disengagement" brought to mind negative images and marginalization; some social gerontologists preferred "active aging" for a time of extension of life expectancy in good health. As old age came to be separated from retirement, the "third age" took on a different meaning; a "fourth age" emerged as a time of loss and fragility. As Guillemard put it, there was a deinstitutionalization of the life course and destandardization of individual paths to old age. Progress in longevity was accompanied by considerable shortening of the working life. It was becoming common to see, out of four generations, two retired, one in school, and only one at work (Guillemard, p. 19). But national differences mattered. The employment rate for Europeans over 55 was 35–39%, for Japanese almost 70% (p. 24). She saw a particularly fragile situation for French workers in their 50s but increased rates of senior employment in the Netherlands and Finland (p. 97). Sweden developed reeducation for continued employment and Japan raised its retirement age. The age of right to a pension went gradually from 60 to 65 (pp. 164–165). Salaried workers had an obligation to remain active, and employers had an obligation to assure opportunities for work.

Some social gerontologists, inspired in some cases by Laslett's idea of the third age, called for a much more flexible system in which people might take sabbaticals from careers and return at later ages. Flexible plans would permit temporary withdrawals and active aging. Gerontologists might still address issues of retirement, but their attention was shifting to the 4th age, much later life, and matters of dependency and autonomy. They look at morale, life satisfaction, and mental functioning in different environments for aging (Gubrium, *Late Life*). Common themes are the physical space occupied by the elderly, whether at home or in retirement or nursing homes, the access to family, community, provisions and resources. For some gerontologists the spiritual was as important as the physical. But the physical can extend beyond issues of housing to matters of urban neighborhood, transportation networks, technology, and the meaning of home. The city may pose particular challenges but, with smart design and adaptation, may be better suited to the aged than country or suburb (Chapon).

Migration has emerged as another theme in social gerontology, not only the decision to move to an adult child's home or to an institution, but also the decision upon retirement to move to a warmer climate, Florida or Arizona for many Americans, France or Spain for English elders. Studies of North African immigrant aging in European cities indicate an initial desire to return to the home country. As people establish new homes and see their children settle more permanently, this becomes a more unusual practice, although there has continued to be a desire among elders to be buried in the country of origin.

Historicizing the migration of various groups to the aging countries of Europe requires an appreciation not only of the flow of labor across the globe in the late twentieth and early twenty-first centuries. It also encourages a look back half a century, when labor shortages in a Europe recovering from the Second World War stimulated immigration from former colonies. At first the assumption was that new immigrants from outside Europe would work temporarily and then return to their places of origin. A recent government report in France refers to the "myth of the return." In part it was a function of French desires not to have to incorporate newcomers into French society (despite the fact that, after the United States, they had been the largest recipient of immigrants in the late nineteenth and early twentieth centuries—mostly European immigrants, of course). But the myth also stands for the desires of migrants themselves. Many held out hopes of returning, and male migrants greatly outnumbered females. By the 1970s it became evident that the immigrant population was more permanently settled. And as the population aged, it found itself facing a double challenge. Not only did older immigrants have to deal with many of the challenges that characterized old age for the majority; they also had to deal with a challenge to their self-images. They had come precisely to work; adjusting to retirement and a majority culture of leisure was unexpected (*Une vieillesse digne pour les immigrés âgés*).

Other themes taken up by social gerontologists were aging and sexuality, including questions of whether men and women were growing more like one another, the gender paradox of women outliving men but being in worse health, the importance of generation or cohort experience in aging, and different rates of aging resulting from different kinds of work. Thus, class inequalities might extend into old age, and retirement was valued in diverse ways. Work at home that had been designated women's work continued long past retirement (Legrand and Voléry). But some forms of "women's work" also continued outside the home. Aline Charles' study of aging among mostly female workers in large Montreal hospitals in the mid-twentieth century reveals that while some women (employees) followed a pattern that resembled that of men, others continued working either as members of religious orders or as volunteers. Thus, one group of women could be said to have followed a structured form of aging and retirement while others experienced the same chronological ages as individuals, choosing to work or not.

Some sociologists took up themes of kinship and generation. Solidarities could occur within and across generations. Blended families provided new opportunities and challenges for different generations, and gay and lesbian populations often found themselves in a period of change from greater solidarity within age cohorts to intergenerational family structures that paralleled those of the majority. Grandparents saw their roles evolve as their adult children had children with different partners. To what extent did religion shape intergenerational relations? How was the role of caregiving evolving? Methodologically, how could one tease apart age, period, and cohort effects on life? Advancing age may have one effect, historical events another, and the succession of cohorts yet another (Silverstein and Giarrusso).

One theme that has seen considerable development in social gerontology as practiced around the world is that of exclusion (and inclusion). It provides a way of talking about economic, political, and social contexts. Scholars focus on domains of social exclusion "from material resources, social relations, civic activities, basic services, and neighbourhoods" (Keating and Scharf, p. 163).

Sociologists of health and disease have had much to say about aging. Laëtitia Ngatcha-Ribert's *Alzheimer: la construction sociale d'une maladie* looks at the different actors who participated in the social construction of the disease that has come to signify advanced age in the Western world. Medical research is one part of the story. Scientists had distinguished between Alzheimer's, which was a way of designating one kind of early-onset dementia, and dementias in advanced age. Yet, as it became increasingly difficult to distinguish between these types, it was possible to see a process of Alzheimerization of old age. Paradoxically, the increasing health of old people became masked by the fears that Alzheimer's lay in everyone's future (either as patient or caregiver). The story involves the work of neurologists, psychologists, psychiatrists, and geriatricians as well as the public, including families of patients, and governments. Medical sociologists see a particular combination of fright and comfort in the Western world. Those who have studied China and India have found various ways in which people normalize behaviors that in the West would be identified with disease. A change in cognitive ability and even a kind of "childishness" might be seen as natural results of aging. One could be ill but not diseased. But the professions involved with Alzheimer's as well as pharmaceutical companies saw disease springing up everywhere.

Alzheimer's disease has been one topic of concern for psychologists interested in aging, but it's only one. Paul and Margret Baltes, reacting against views of old age as unrelenting decline, developed ideas of "successful aging" and "Selective Optimization with Compensation (SOC)." Like a number of other gerontologists and psychologists, they were concerned with competence, dependence, and autonomy. Margret M. Baltes' *The Many Faces of Dependency in Old Age* looks at "learned dependency." She sees gain as well as loss in certain forms of dependency.

> In old age with its diverse losses, dependency, although possibly hastening decline, might be an optimizing strategy in that it initiates and secures social contact. Moreover, dependency might have a compensatory function in that it allows the elderly to conserve energy and, therefore, to engage in more desirable activities.
>
> *(p. xv)*

Behavioral dependency might simply result in learned helplessness, an overly pampering environment resulting in a "dependency-support script" (p. 4). Intervention can lead to overcare and a loss of independence. Baltes argues that "environments can be changed to promote an independence-support script" (*Ibid.*). But self-selected behavioral dependency is seen as part of successful aging. It encourages autonomy and choice and can be seen as part of selection with compensation.

One of the themes that carries over from philosophical treatments of aging is that of narrative. How do people turn their lives into coherent stories? Christian Lalive d'Epinay, a Swiss psychologist, has written (sometimes alone, sometimes with such colleagues as Stefano Cavalli) about this question in the context of the emergence of the 4th age, which became a major theme in the 1980s. He suggests that that terminology, which is characteristic of European gerontology, emphasizes the experience of individuals, while the American use of the term "old old" places the emphasis on a demographic group. For Lalive d'Epinay, the life course (*parcours de vie*) is the subject, and he has collected life histories to see how individuals deal with aging in a subjective way. They become characters analogous to literary ones, but characters created by themselves, and they have something to say about the passage of time and the meaning of their lives. This is one area where gerontology allows a view of the aging subject, rethinking or rewriting his or her life, recognizing change but asserting one's identity and achieving equilibrium. He and Cavalli also build upon the Baltes' work on dependency. From a sample of people in their 80s and 90s, they sketch out various trajectories of life, finding 10–15% of people remaining independent right up to death, 5% going suddenly from independence to dependence, and the vast majority (80–85%) going through a period of "fragility." Of that majority, half never become dependent (Lalive d'Epinay and Cavalli, pp. 25–27). Thus, Lalive d'Epinay and Cavalli encounter people who will say they're aged but not old, and their interviews reveal people who associate becoming old with one particular moment or a more gradual process. Such a psychological approach to aging complements sociological studies that speak of *déprise*, a willing detachment, a selective retreat rather than total disengagement. People may decide to concentrate on certain aspects of their lives and certain neighborhood spaces (Clément and Membrado).

The emphasis on narrative results from attention to the environmental and institutional spaces the aged occupy, elders' desire to tell their own stories, and gerontologists' willingness to listen. The work of the gerontologist is then akin to that of the ethnographer or the oral historian. The "expert" has some idea of how to order things and considerable knowledge of the field, but the informant exercises considerable control in giving shape to the aging self. Sociologists Jaber Gubrium and James Holstein have produced several volumes of qualitative studies that frequently allow elders' voices to come through. Among them are *Aging and Everyday Life*, *Ways of Aging*, and the aptly named *The Self We Live By*.

Some of the qualitative social scientific literature has reached the general public. Indeed, oral histories by Ronald Blythe (*The View in Winter*) and Studs Terkel (*Coming of Age*) have reached large numbers of readers interested in hearing the voices of the aged. And scholars and journalists like Barbara Myerhoff (*Number Our Days*) and Tracy Kidder (*Old Friends*) report on lives in senior centers or residential institutions. Other professions have found a general readership on aging. Physicians like Sherwin Nuland in the United States or Maurice Tubiana in France summarize the biological and phenomenological processes of aging and offer advice about remaining active and healthy. Both emphasize the maintenance of social ties. Tubiana, a cancer specialist in Paris, calls for self-confidence, feeling useful and capable of helping others, and enjoying being helped by others (*Le bien-vieillir: la révolution de l'âge*). Richard Posner's *Aging and Old Age* brings the gravitas of a judge and a knowledge of both philosophy and economics to his treatment of age and aging, and economist Peter Peterson's *Gray Dawn: How the Coming Age Wave Will Transform America—and the World*, while not casting as wide a net as the others, combines demography and economics to issue a warning about what lies ahead. His is the message that sometimes crowds out more optimistic visions.

One increasingly popular genre in the late twentieth and twenty-first centuries is that of memoir, often written from the perspective of advanced age. Sometimes they have a literary cast, as in Malcolm Cowley's *The View from Eighty*; often they tell a story of persistence. Betty Friedan's takes that form (*The Fountain of Age*), a way of bringing to aging the critical, activist sense that informed her earlier work on feminism. But as Ruth Ray points out, Friedan's depiction of continued vitality has very little to say about the 4th age or old old. Indeed, feminist writings on age have tended to emphasize midlife or postmenopausal experience (Calasanti and Slevin). Their strength has been to focus on certain issues of embodiment. This has been useful in terms of gender difference and minority forms of sexuality.

More than books, mass media in general, from newspapers and magazines to television, radio, and online platforms, have reached large numbers of people on issues of retirement and old age. Among the most frequently emailed articles from the *New York Times* in recent years have been those devoted to aging. They often take on the optimistic tone of "healthy aging," but they also offer warnings about the consequences of falls. Some provide moving narratives about aging and caregiving.

One of the most striking genres has been the one in which a Western observer or an immigrant who lives and works in the West, compares aging across cultures. It had been common, as was the case in some social science literature, to idealize other ways of growing old. But increasingly, these writings seek to downplay any perceived non-Western advantage. In several cases, journalists have borrowed the line from Yeats's poem "Sailing to Byzantium," which begins, "No country for old men." Or perhaps they are borrowing from the Cormac McCarthy novel or the Coen Brothers movie. On July 30, 2010, Sandip Roy's "India: No Country for Old People?" gave National Public Radio audiences a view of aging in India in which one of the subjects was his mother. On February 19, 2013, Mark W. Frazier's "No Country for Old Age" described in the *New York Times* the looming pension crisis in China. Another *Times* article, appearing on July 3, 2013, by Edward Wong, "A Chinese Virtue is Now the Law," described a law on the "Protection of the Rights and Interests of Elderly People" that "lay out the duties of children and their obligation to tend to the 'spiritual needs of the elderly'." The message seemed to be that those countries that were renowned for revering the elderly were doing no better than the rest of us, maybe worse. Perhaps this was a way of making Western readers feel better. In any case, such articles do make the world seem smaller, as it must feel for Americans flying "home" to India to check in on aged parents. So we see a kind of convergence.

Convergence is one story. Diversity is another. American gerontology in the first instance and international gerontology subsequently took up the theme of diversity in a big way. American gerontologists, tending to issues of ethnicity and class, were already saying in the 1970s that the national population is too diverse to permit generalization. And the early twenty-first-century concern for socio-economic inequality has implications for the life course and the last years of life. So the paradox is that we recognize greater diversity while also recognizing a common humanity in experiencing aging.

As early as the 1970s, American scholarship in gerontology was beginning to pay some attention to race and ethnicity. It was still largely wedded to the modernization narrative and assumptions that cultures undergoing rapid change would see diminished status for the elderly, but authors of that era often claimed to see persistent roles and values among ethnic minorities that would benefit elders. The assumption was that respect and family support were more important than individualism. In treating immigrant communities that had developed since the late nineteenth century, scholars often identified the aged as providing stability and exercising authority. Family members and communities were said to provide support for elders, and small businesses in cities catered to particular immigrant groups. Cultural connections to places of origin were sometimes maintained. Even studies of African Americans, whose arrival occurred much earlier and under much different circumstances, drew long-term connections with cultural values of respect for elders that went back to the west coast of Africa.

Ethnic elders confronted modernity not only in the outside world but, crucially, in their own families, as children and grandchildren balanced family ties against the pull of economic opportunities, suburban neighborhoods, and other parts of the country. When Donald E. Gelfand took up the generational issue in *Aging: The Ethnic Factor* in 1982 he could claim that immigrants were now headed directly to the suburbs (Gelfand, 1982, p. 88). More recently, in quite a few American cities, the situation seems even more like that of a hundred years ago, as large urban neighborhoods absorb waves of immigrants. The latest arrivals bring to mind the oft-told tale of late-nineteenth and early-twentieth-century immigration involving, for example, aging in Polish- and Italian-American neighborhoods, as younger people moved on (pp. 90–98). Adult children were less willing to house aged parents, and ethnic identity showed signs of decline. Of course, one shouldn't exaggerate. Immigrant families were often more extended than others because it was too impractical or too expensive to set up independent households (p. 104). Once they could afford to break away, younger generations did, and many elders began to favor continued independence themselves, but individual intergenerational relationships could be characterized by what gerontologist Leopold Rosenmayr termed "intimacy at a distance."

This was no less true for increasing numbers of Mexican American families in the late twentieth century as it was for earlier waves of immigrants from eastern and southern Europe. Still, each group has its own story; better, each group has multiple stories. More highly educated and wealthier migrants maintain their own sorts of global ties. Ethnic aging among poorer immigrants may appear rather more traditional, including tales of travel itself, a search for security, and family and church support. Many groups faced similar challenges of poverty and discrimination, but each had a somewhat different story to tell. Among Italian Americans it was a story of tension between patriarchal authority and the pull of American individualism. When a scholar suggests that the "ability to express affect and emotions allows the family and the older person to give expression to their feelings about the family hierarchy as well as family obligations" and that therefore the elders' authority was maintained, one is grateful for the attempt to get at people's feelings but wonders whether cultural stereotyping is at work (Gelfand, 1994, p. 60). Hybrid identities create important complications.

Individual ethnic groups in US cities faced the challenges of urban life, but some arrived with urban experience, and some created social welfare institutions to compensate for being shut out of existing ones. Catholic and Jewish hospitals and old age homes continued to cater to neighborhoods even after the founding groups had largely moved to the suburbs or other parts of the country. But some suburbanites left their elders in urban neighborhoods that offered familiarity and a sense of community. Again, generalization would be hazardous.

There was a time when historians emphasized discontinuity in the African American experience. Slavery and forced migration followed by freedom and the search for equality meant extraordinary change. But some cultural continuities and global interactions provided a sense of continuity. Those who have written on African American history see continuity from the Jim Crow era deep into the twentieth century, whether in terms of discrimination or resistance through family, school, and church. Family poverty, low-wage jobs, and comparatively low access to pensions were important factors in the experience of the Black elderly. Inequality was starkly evident in rates of life expectancy. Even in the late twentieth century, the differential between White and Black life expectancy at birth was six years for women and seven years for men. Presumably, the combination of low-wage work in hazardous conditions, substandard housing, and unequal access to medical care caused earlier aging. Yet, there came a period of crossover in life expectancy. If they reached their early 70s, Blacks could expect to outlive Whites. It's not clear why, but we do know that different groups suffered differently from particular diseases. Black male mortality from stroke was three times that of Whites at ages 55–64; but there would be a crossover effect at higher ages. In general, Black elders reported worse health than Whites, but they also reported greater satisfaction in retirement. Perhaps that's a reflection of the nature of work among poorer populations and the importance of social security (*Ibid.*, pp. 71–72). Experience and custom matter, and recent study indicates a stronger sense of obligation toward elderly parents among African Americans than either Whites or Caribbean Blacks (Jackson, Brown, Antonucci, and Daatland, p. 479).

American Indian aging shares characteristics with later-arriving ethnic groups' experience. There was significant movement to urban areas in the 1980s so that by the early 1990s (Gelfand, 1994, p. 78) only a quarter lived on reservations, with the balance evenly divided between city and country. Comparing reservation and urban Indians, Gelfand wrote, "A return to the reservation can resolve some split family issues and result in an 'economically efficient life career strategy' for older American Indians." Urban elders faced financial challenges, isolation, and a lack of social services (p. 79). A survey by the National Indian Council on Aging (1981) indicated signs of premature aging. Poverty and alcoholism were among the key factors, but since then life expectancy among the Navajos, for example, has risen dramatically. "Across the country the indicated decline in mortality among Native Americans has been matched by an increase in chronic illnesses, which mirrors the picture among the older population in the United States" (p. 83).

Cultural values of respect for elders survived and in some cases were strengthened. In the face of rapid change in recent times, elders found they might restore some of their authority as bearers of traditions that younger community members were coming to appreciate. One example is the renewed interest in Ojibwe religion as encouraging authority and honor (McNally).

Studies of Latino aging looked at some of the same issues as studies of other groups. They included family support, migration, religious institutions, and health. Spanish Harlem in New York City has been the setting for studies of aging, work, and social connections as well as of Puerto Rican grandmothers who have found themselves raising grandchildren, something that can be seen both as a challenge and as an essential part of older women's identities. While the Latino population remains relatively young, it will eventually age more rapidly than others. Of course, Latino populations come from a very wide range of places, their cultural practices are hardly uniform, and their health profiles are divergent. Some groups have been better studied than others. One early study devoted to Mexican Americans anticipated a theme that was largely overlooked: political participation and engagement.

Fernando M. Torres-Gil observed in the early 1980s that Mexican American elders, although politically inactive themselves, were aware of political issues and supportive of younger activists. Those born in the US were much more active then first-generation immigrants. Urban elders and those in New Mexico, where Spanish speakers were established well before English speakers, were among the leaders. It is possible to trace the development of Hispanic activism on aging issues following a bit behind national organizations. Hispanics were not included in the 1971 White House Conference on Aging, but the First National Conference on the Spanish-speaking Elderly and the founding of the Asociación Nacional Pro Personas Mayores in 1975 meant inclusion in the 1981 White House Conference. Another way that Latinos and particularly Latinas (not particularly Mexican American) became involved in aging issues was through work in social services and healthcare professions. Awareness spread of premature aging and mortality in Hispanic communities, and an earlier generation's attempt to assimilate by downplaying ethnic identity gave way to a newer generation's discovery of culture and heritage (Torres-Gil, 1982). More recent studies by Torres-Gil and others reveal a large array of ethnic-based groups focusing on aging and higher rates of voting by elders than by younger people from the same groups (Torres-Gil, 2005).

Examples in the preceding paragraphs are drawn from experiences in the United States, but ethnic aging is also being explored elsewhere, as among the already mentioned Bangladeshi elders in London and Iranian elders in Sweden whose views of successful aging changed in going from place to place as they applied different cultural norms in different contexts (Torres). In both of these examples, it was possible for aging individuals to select from among various cultural models linked to place of origin, mother tongue, or religious tradition. They might also have adopted what they perceived to be majority ideas of aging.

Recognition of ethnic cultural identity within Western societies paralleled what was going on in the wider world in terms of adaptation or cultural resistance to contemporary modern and post-modern prescriptions for aging. Thus, for people in many parts of the world, Confucianism, Hinduism, and African traditions, while rarely if ever characterizing "whole" societies in the past and often presented retrospectively from Western points of view, offered models of wisdom and cultural grounds for resistance. One wonders about the strength of such resistance in the decades to come, when demographers predict the most rapid aging among many of these same groups and a kind of convergence around a common fate. Recent work on the survival of forms of filial piety in contexts of financial and emotional pressure in East Asia suggests flexibility, compromise, and a desire to update strained traditions. Indeed, recognition of people's hybrid identities has led to a serious critique of older ethnic studies as offering too simple a framework for understanding how people see themselves. Demography, culture, and politics are all at play and all intertwined.

When we think of aging and politics, we may think of activist groups like the Gray Panthers, founded in 1970 by Maggie Kuhn, and imitated by groups in Western Europe, or we may think of larger lobbying organizations such as the American Association of Retired Persons (AARP), which reaches out to Americans as they hit age 50 and has been described as the largest lobbying group in American politics. Or we may think of social service organizations that engage in more local political struggles. Older Americans vote in greater percentages than other age groups, and caregivers, whether family members or professionals, have also made their voices heard.

Even in the developed world, environmental emergencies affect the aged in tragic ways. Indeed, it may be a misnomer to call them strictly "environmental," as societal and political choices had important influences. The impact of Hurricane Katrina, which had a well-known differential effect on African Americans in and around New Orleans, was devastating to the aged. And the heat wave that struck Western Europe in August of 2003 revealed a previously "invisible" population of elderly. Doctors and gerontologists in Paris who discussed the event in its aftermath focused on victimization, invisibility, and the elderly's rights as citizens. The doctor who organized the conference spoke of an obligation of "non-abandonment" (Hirsch).

The politics of aging can thus be concerned with local emergencies. But it can also be addressed to problems of ageism, described as comparable to the scourges of racism and sexism. Ageism may take a cultural form, as prejudice against the old may be built into the language of everyday life and images broadcast by the media (Gullette). It may also play a role in conflicts over public policy, employment, pensions, and social security (Macnicol). In very recent times, the shift from defined benefit schemes to defined contribution schemes implies an individualization of risk just as old age has been defined as a global issue (Blackburn). How that works out in the future is partly a function of seniors' (and future seniors') political mobilization.

Today the issues of aging find their way into global political debates. What happens in India, Pakistan, or Bangladesh has repercussions for immigrant families in Britain. Similarly, the politics of Ukraine, Mexico, and the Caribbean matter for transnational populations in the United States. Immigration policies that permit or prevent family reunification have consequences for inclusion and exclusion in old age around the world.

Our voyage across time and space has revealed diverse ways of growing old but also some important commonalities. The themes of aging in the distant past speak to us even today. Classical and medieval cultures offer both wisdom and cautionary tales. The long story of state-making and empire-building has implications for elders. The demographic transitions, whether in Europe a hundred years ago or in Asia and Latin America today, make for dramatic differences in life expectancy and planning. The emergence of 3rd and 4th ages—where the 4th is described in Switzerland as beginning at 80, in India at 70, and the challenges of 3rd-age women caring for 4th-age elders has already been noted in Brazil (Brown)—, pension schemes, and systems of social security have had important impacts on the world's political agendas. The aging self is a subject of history as well as autobiography.

Demographic aging is often viewed through an economic lens. Students of world politics even consider its implications for power relations. Thus, choices are made between military spending and foreign intervention on the one hand and domestic needs on the other, and world powers contemplate their relative fates as their populations grow older. World Bank, CIA, and Center for Strategic and International Studies reports can have significant impacts.

One of the unfortunate discoveries of the late twentieth and early twenty-first centuries is that despite the horrors brought on by nationalism in the modern era, now that the particular ideological conflict of the Cold War has been rendered moot, nationalism and tribalism have surged back. Aging, like climate change, gets bumped by war, extremist religious expression, and nationalism. Differences may be celebrated or may be sources of conflict. The aged may be seen as the "other." Or we may recognize a common humanity in experiencing aging. Will having the same fate lead to mutual recognition, intergenerational and international cooperation, and a better way of growing old? Such questions take us beyond the purview of historians into the future; yet, knowledge of what came before can provide elements of a response.

This book's preface referred to two ways of thinking about aging: "the experience of individuals and the transformation of populations." The latter often seems to overwhelm the former. Contemporary demographic, economic, and political approaches place a strong emphasis on population aging and very big numbers. This history of aging has recognized the importance of those approaches and the changes that mark the modern and contemporary periods. But it has also insisted on the experience of individuals. They have included Roman patriarchs and matrons, Confucian ancestor-worshipers, medieval priests, Australian pensioners, hospitalized Europeans and their doctors, American Civil War veterans, Ugandan grandmothers, and Japanese mothers-in-law. Even if they only received a bare mention, the bibliographical references will lead readers to more detailed and specialized accounts.

The book's attention to historiography, its explicit reliance upon a growing and evolving literature, provides a sense of how historians do their work. Whatever the topic, we rely upon a community of scholars and on those sources that are currently available. The history of aging and the aged, like the field of gerontology, has privileged the experience of the Western world. This book attempts to cover what is already known and to encourage its readers to follow its leads in the direction of a more global history. It also demonstrates that while expertise matters, so do the subjective experiences of ordinary people making their way through history and the life course.

Works Cited and Further Reading

Populations âgées et révolution grise: Les hommes et les sociétés face à leurs vieillissements. Actes du Colloque Chaire Quetelet '86, Louvain-la-Neuve, 6–10 octobre 1986, sous la direction de Michel Loriaux, Dominique Rémy, et Eric Vilquin (Bruxelles: Editions CIACO, 1990); J.F. Fries, "Aging, Natural Death, and the Compression of Morbidity," *The New England Journal of Medicine*, Vol. 303, No. 3 (1980): 130–135; J.F. Fries and L.M. Crapo, *Vitality and Aging: Implications of the Rectangular Curve* (San Francisco: W.H. Freeman and Company, 1981); Peter Uhlenberg, ed., *International Handbook of Population Aging* (Dordrecht: Springer, 2009); Mildred M. Seltzer, *The Impact of Increased Life Expectancy: Beyond the Gray Horizon* (NY: Springer, 1995); Anne-Marie Guillemard, *Les défis du vieillissement: âge, emploi, retraite, perspectives internationales* (Paris: Armand Colin, 2010); Bernd Marin, *Welfare in an Idle Society? Reinventing Retirement, Work, Wealth, Health, and Welfare. A Primer on Re-Designing Social Security to Cope with Global Ageing and 21st Century Pension Future: Austria as a Case in Point*, European Center Vienna (Farnham and Burlington: Ashgate Publishing Company, 2013); "The Autopilot Solution," in *The Economist*, February 2, 2013.

Peter Laslett and James Fishkin, eds., *Justice Between Age Groups and Generations* (New Haven: Yale UP, 1992); Daniel Callahan, *Setting Limits: Medical Goals in an Aging Society* (NY: Simon and Schuster, 1987); Norman Daniels, *Am I My Parents' Keeper?* (Oxford: Oxford UP, 1988); Richard Posner, *Aging and Old Age* (Chicago: University of Chicago Press, 1995); Dennis McKerlie, "Justice Between the Young and the Old," *Philosophy and Public Affairs*, Vol. 30, No. 2 (April 2001): 152–177) and *Justice Between the Young and the Old* (Oxford: Oxford UP, 2012); Angieszka Jaworska, "Respecting the Margins of Agency: Alzheimer's Patients and the Capacity to Value, *Philosophy and Public Affairs*, Vol. 28, No. 2 (1999): 105–138. One of the best guides to philosophical debates on aging is Helen Small, *The Long Life* (Oxford: Oxford UP, 2007).

Jaber Gubrium, ed., *Late Life: Communities and Environmental Policy* (Springfield, IL: Charles C. Thomas, 1974); Pierre-Marie Chapon, *Bâtir une ville pour tous les âges* (Paris: La Documentation française, 2013); *Une vieillesse digne pour les immigrés âgés: un défi à relever en urgence*. Rapport d'information no. 1214 (Paris: Assemblée Nationale, July 2013). On the dilemma of the aged immigrant, see Philippe Pitaud, Brigitte Dherbey, and Daïba Lazreug, "Contribution à une réflexion sur la condition des immigrés âgés," in Philippe Pitaud and Richard Vercauteren, eds., *Vieillir dans les villes de l'Europe du sud: Comparaisons et échanges internationaux* (Ramonville: Érès, 1994), pp. 173–193.

Monique Legrand and Ingrid Voléry, eds., *Genre et parcours de vie: vers une nouvelle police des corps et des âges?* (Nancy: Presses universitaires de Nancy, 2013); Aline Charles, *Quand devient-on vieille? Femmes, âge et travail au Québec, 1940–1980* (Québec: Les presses de l'Université Laval, 2007); Merril Silverstein and Roseann Giarrusso, eds., *Kinship and Cohort in an Aging Society: From Generation to Generation* (Baltimore: Johns Hopkins UP, 2013); Norah Keating and Thomas Scharf, "Revisiting Social Exclusion of Older Adults," chapter 10 in Thomas Scharf and Norah C. Keating, eds., *From Exclusion to Inclusion in Old Age: A Global Challenge* (Bristol and Chicago: Policy Press, 2012); Laëtitia Ngatcha-Ribert, *Alzheimer: la construction sociale d'une maladie* (Paris: Dunod, 2012); Paul B. Baltes and Margret M. Baltes, eds., *Successful Aging: Perspectives from the Behavioral Sciences* (Cambridge: Cambridge UP, 1990); Margret M. Baltes, *The Many Faces of Dependency in Old Age* (Cambridge: Cambridge UP, 1996); Christian Lalive d'Epinay and Stefano Cavalli, *Le quatrième âge ou la dernière étape de la vie* (Lausanne: Presses polytechniques et universitaires romandes, 2013); Serge Clément and Monique Membrado, "Expériences du vieillir: généalogie de la notion de déprise," in Sylvie Carbonnelle, ed., *Penser les vieillesses: Regards sociologiques et anthropologiques sur l'avancée en âge* (Paris: Seli Arslan, 2010), pp. 109–128; Jaber Gubrium and James Holstein, *Aging and Everyday Life* (Malden, MA and Oxford: Blackwell, 2000), *Ways of Aging* (Malden, MA and Oxford: Blackwell, 2003), and *The Self We Live By* (NY: Oxford University Press, 2000).

Ronald Blythe, *The View in Winter: Reflections on Old Age* (NY: Harcourt Brace Jovanovich, 1979); Studs Terkel, *Coming of Age: Growing Up in the Twentieth Century* (NY: The New Press, 1995); Barbara Myerhoff, *Number Our Days* (NY: E.P. Dutton, 1979); Tracy Kidder, *Old Friends* (Boston: Houghton Mifflin, 1993); Sherwin B. Nuland, *The Art of Aging: A Doctor's Prescription for Well-Being* (NY: Random House, 2007); Maurice Tubiana, *Le bien-vieillir: la révolution de l'âge*, 2nd edition, (Paris: Editions de Fallois, 2007); Richard Posner, *Aging and Old Age* (Chicago: University of Chicago Press, 1995); Peter Peterson, *Gray Dawn: How the Coming Age Wave Will Transform America—and the World* (NY: Crown, 1999); Malcolm Cowley, *The View from Eighty* (NY: Viking Press, 1980); Betty Friedan, *The Fountain of Age* (NY: Simon and Schuster, 1993), and see Ruth Ray's critique, "The Personal as Political: The Legacy of Betty Friedan," in Toni M.

Calasanti and Kathleen F. Slevin, eds., *Age Matters: Realigning Feminist Thinking* (NY: Routledge, 2008).
Jon Hendricks, ed., *In the Country of the Old* (NY: Baywood, 1979); Donald E. Gelfand, *Aging: The Ethnic Factor* (Boston: Little, Brown, 1982), and *Aging and Ethnicity: Knowledge and Services* (NY: Springer, 1994); James S. Jackson, Edna Brown, Toni C. Antonucci, and Svein Olav Daatland, "Ethnic Diversity in Ageing, Multicultural Societies," in *The Cambridge Handbook of Age and Ageing*, edited by Malcolm L. Johnson, in association with Vern L. Bengston, Peter G. Coleman, and Thomas B.L. Kirkwood (Cambridge: Cambridge UP, 2005); Michael David McNally, *Honoring Elders: Aging, Authority, and Ojibwe Religion* (NY: Columbia UP, 2009); Judith Noemi Freidenberg, *Growing Old in El Barrio* (NY: New York University Press, 2000); Marta B. Rodríguez-Galán, "Grandmothering in Life-Course Perspective: A Study of Puerto Rican Grandmothers Raising Grandchildren in the United States," chapter 9 in *Transitions and Transformations: Cultural Perspectives on Aging and the Life Course*, edited by Caitrin Lynch and Jason Danely (NY and Oxford: Berghahn Books, 2013); Fernando M. Torres-Gil, *Politics of Aging among Elder Hispanics* (Washington: University Press of America, 1982), and "Ageing and Public Policy in Ethnically Diverse Societies," in *The Cambridge Handbook of Age and Ageing*, edited by Malcolm L. Johnson, in association with Vern L. Bengston, Peter G. Coleman, and Thomas B.L. Kirkwood (Cambridge: Cambridge UP, 2005), pp. 670–681; Sandra Torres, "Understandings of Successful Ageing in the Context of Migration: The Case of Iranian Immigrants in Sweden," *Ageing and Society*, Vol. 21 (2001): 333–355. For the connection between aging and migration, particularly as care-givers are concerned, see Sjaak Van Der Geest, Anke Mul and Hans Vermeulen, "Linkages between Migration and the Care of Frail Older People: Observations from Greece, Ghana and the Netherlands," *Ageing and Society*, Vol. 24 (2004): 431–450.

Vieillesses méconnues: enjeux éthiques de la crise d'août 2003, 6e colloque d'éthique de Bicêtre, 3 octobre 2003, Faculté de médecine Paris-Sud 11, edited by Emmanuel Hirsch (Paris: Assistance publique–Hôpitaux de Paris, Espace éthique, 2004); Margaret Morganroth Gullette, *Agewise: Fighting the New Ageism in America* (Chicago: University of Chicago Press, 2011); John Macnicol, *Age Discrimination: An Historical and Contemporary Analysis* (Cambridge: Cambridge University Press, 2006); Robin Blackburn, *Banking on Death, Or Investing in Life: The History and Future of Pensions* (London: Verso, 2002), and *Age Shock: How Finance is Failing Us* (London: Verso, 2006); Diana De G. Brown, "'I Have to Stay Healthy:' Elder Caregiving and the Third Age in a Brazilian Community," chapter 8 in *Transitions and Transformations*.

Mark L. Haas, "A Geriatric Peace? The Future of U.S. Power in a World of Aging Populations," *International Security*, Vol. 32, No. 1 (Summer 2007): 112–147; The World Bank, *Averting the Old Age Crisis: Policies to Protect the Old and Promote Growth* (NY: Oxford University Press, 1994); Central Intelligence Agency, "Long-Term Global Demographic Trends: Reshaping the Geopolitical

Landscape" (July 2001), https://www.cia.gov/library/reports/general-reports-1/Demo_Trends_For_Web.pdf; Richard Jackson, *The Global Retirement Crisis: The Threat to World Stability and What to Do About It* (Washington, DC: Center for Strategic and International Studies, 2002); Thomas Scharf and Norah Keating, eds., *From Exclusion to Inclusion in Old Age: A Global Challenge* (Bristol: Policy Press, 2012).

INDEX

AARP 141
Aboderin, Isabella 111
Ache 11
Achenbaum, W. Andrew 5, 6, 71, 72
Adarkar, B.P. 122
Africa 89, 90–93; age-sets in 12; contemporary 111–13; hunter-gatherers in 10, 11; *see also individual countries*
African Americans 89, 138, 139
age and public office 20, 30, 46, 50
ageism 141
ages of life xi, 29, 30, 44–5, 51, 52; African 90; Aztec 88; Confucian 20, 22; Mesopotamian 24
aging: contemporary 127–46; and culture 5–6, 10; demographic xiii, 3–4, 74–8, 97, 107–14, 127, 128–30, 142; and economics 136; and environment 123, 133, 141; and gender 6, 9, 10, 12, 52, 72, 113, 134; historiography of xi-xv, 3–8; master narratives of xi-xii; and politics 141–2; and property 6, 9, 13, 25; and space 133, 136
agriculture 12, 68, 84, 90
Alborn, Timothy 83
alcohol 24, 88, 108, 116, 139
American Civil War 81
American Revolution 62, 70
Ames, Herbert Brown 121
Amoss, Pamela 16–17
Anglo-Boer War 91
anthropology and aging xii, 6, 9–15, 16

Argentina 113, 124
Aristotle 28, 32, 45
Asia xiii, 16, 77; central 108; east 97; *see also individual countries*
Atlantic Charter 92
Atlee, Clement 85
Augustine, Saint 44
Australia 75–6, 96–7, 131
Austria 81, 130
authority 4–5, 12, 28–30, 33–34, 39, 88, 138
Avicenna 46, 117
Ayurveda 18, 19, 93, 117
Aztecs 88, 116

Bá, Amadou Hepâté 90
Bacon, Francis 53, 59, 117
Bacon, Roger 46
Baltes, Paul and Margret 135
Banner, Lois 6
Baruya 12
Bauer, Ennio 27–8
Beauvoir, Simone de 9, 23, 127, 132
Bede 44
Belgium 128
Bengalis 110–111
Bengston, Vern L. 123
Bernard, Claude 119
Bernardino of Siena 45
Beveridge Report (1942) 84, 92, 122
Bhagavad Gita 17–18
Bible 26, 40, 43, 44, 54

Bismarck, Otto von 83
Black Death 48–9
Blythe, Ronald 136
Boccaccio 49
bodily decline 113, 116, 118; and Buddhism 19; and Confucianism 22; and Hinduism 17; and Islam 43; and medicine 118–20; medieval 45; Renaissance 51–3; Roman 29–33
Boerhaave, Herman 117
Bois, Jean-Pierre 67–8, 70, 71
Booth, Charles 83, 121
Bosnia-Herzegovina 108
Botelho, L.A. 5, 6, 60–1
Botswana 11, 111
Bourdelais, Patrice 7
Brazil 10, 113–14
Brown-Séquard, Charles-Édouard 119
Buddhism 18, 19
Buffon, Georges-Louis Leclerc, comte de 117
bureaucracy 82, 93
Burundi 92

Callahan, Daniel 131
Calvinism 72
Canada 87, 134
capitalism xiii, 57, 82
Cardone, Caroline Schuster 52
Cartier, Michel 23–4
Caspari, Rachel 11
Catholics 88, 139
Caucasus 108
Center for Strategic and International Studies 142
Chamberlain, Joseph 83
Charcot, Jean-Martin 118–19
Chile 101, 113
China: ancient 16, 18–24; contemporary 77, 109–10; European image of 89; influence of 39–40; matrilineal descent in southern 12; medicine in ancient 116–17; revolutionary 93; understanding of dementia in 135
Christianity xiii, 27, 34, 39, 44, 93; and colonialism 89–90; medieval 47–8, 117; Reformation-era 50, 57–9
Chudacoff, Howard 6
CIA 142
Cicero 16, 127; *De Senectute* 31, 34, 43, 67
classical civilizations 16–36
Codex Mendoza 88
Cohen, Lawrence 13, 111
Cokayne, Karen 30–3

Cole, Thomas 5–6, 71–2, 123
colonialism 87–95
commedia dell'arte 51
compression of morbidity 128
Confucianism 16, 19–23, 39–40, 93, 108, 127, 141
Conrad, Christoph 83
Counter-Reformation 50
Cowley, Malcolm 136
Cowper, Sarah, Lady 58
Cribier, Françoise 101
cultural representations xi, 5–6, 32, 41, 45, 51–3, 70–2
Cultural Revolution (China) 93
Czechoslovakia 108

Daniels, Norman 131
death 11, 21, 26–7, 41, 88–9, 108, 111
deferred benefit 101
defined contribution 101, 131
dementia 33; *see also* disease, Alzheimer's
demographic bonus 113
demographic transitions 74–8, 130, 142
demography, Roman 30
Denmark 131
dependency 136
Descartes, René 53, 59, 117
detachment 136
disease 89–90, 139; Alzheimer's 120, 132, 134–5
disengagement 132
Dobe !Kung 11
Durán, Diego 88
Dworkin, Ronald 131

Egypt: ancient 25–6, 116–17; early Coptic Christians in 34; modern 44, 113
elders 24, 26, 90, 111; and knowledge or wisdom 10, 12, 28, 33
England: demographic transition in 75, 77; early modern 58–60; immigrants in 140; literature in 51; medieval 46–7, medicine in 119; pensions in 81–4
England, Robert Stowe 109
Enlightenment 62, 67, 74
Enuma Elish 25
Epic of Gilgamesh 24–5
Erasmus 53
Erny, Pierre 90
ethnicity 137–9
Europe 96; east central 50–1, 108; northwestern 68; *see also individual countries* exclusion 134

Falkner, Thomas 29
family 13, 41–2, 49
Feller, Elise 83
feminism 136–7
Ferguson, James 112
fertility 75–6; decline 113
filial piety, 19–24, 93, 141
Finland 132
First World War 84, 91
Fischer, David Hackett 5
Flanagan, James G. 10
Florentine Codex 88
Foucault, Michel 118
"fourth age" (or old old): absence in feminist studies 137; anticipation of idea of 24; in contemporary gerontology 123, 132–3, 135, 142
fragility 125, 136
France: contemporary 131–3; demographic transition in 75, 77; early modern xii, 60; hospitals in 59; pensions in 81–2, 84
Franco-Prussian War (1870–71) 77, 84
French Revolution 49, 62, 69, 81–2
Friedan, Betty 136–7
friendly societies 61, 82–3
Fries, J.F. 128

Galen 33, 46, 117; Galenic medicine 51, 93
Gardner, Katy 111
Gelfand, Donald E. 138–9
geriatrics 116–122
Germany 77, 83–4, 119
gerontocracy 10, 27, 50, 51, 93
gerontology xii, 116, 118, 120–5, 133–6
gerousiai 27–28
Ghana 111
globalization 87, 107–15
Godelier, Maurice 12
Gourdon, Vincent 6, 70–1
grandparents 6; ancient Chinese 23; contemporary 134; eighteenth-and-nineteenth-century 68, 70–1; in naming practices in Arab family 42; in prehistory 11; Puerto Rican in New York 140; Roman 30; Russian 108; South African 92; Ugandan 112–13
Gratton, Brian 5
Gray Panthers 141
Great Depression 84, 98–9, 101
Greece 16, 27–31
Gubrium, Jaber 136

Guillemard, Anne-Marie 100, 101, 129, 130, 132
Guinea 12, 92
Gutton, Jean-Pierre 67–8

Haber, Carole 5, 119
Hall, G. Stanley 121
Harrell, Stevan 16–17
Harris, Rivkah 24–5
Haycock, Francis Boyd 53
Hebrews 26–7, 40
Hinduism 16, 17, 40, 93, 110, 141
Hippocrates 16, 29, 33, 117
HIV/AIDS 112–13
Holstein, James 136
Hong Kong 93, 108–9
honor xi, 13, 16, 22–3, 26–8, 31, 40, 41, 88
Horace 32
hospitals 18, 47, 52–3, 59, 69, 73
Hugo, Victor 70
Hungary 50–1, 108

India: aging and gerontology in 122; ancient 17–19; colonial influence on 84, 89; early medicine in 116–17, modern 102, 110–11; understanding of dementia in 135
Indians, North American 13–14, 88–90, 139–40
individualism 70, 84
industrialization 62
insurance 82, 83
intergenerational justice 131–2
intergenerational relations: in Africa 111–12; conflict over public policy 101; in contemporary societies 127, 134, 138; in Egypt 25; in French Revolutionary era 69; medieval 48; and property 68; in Renaissance 51; and welfare state 97
intergenerational solidarity 84, 110
Inuit 11
Iranians in Sweden 140
Isenberg, Sheldon 26
Isidore of Seville 44
Islam xiii, 18, 40–4, 90, 93, 108
Italian Americans 138
Italy 49, 131

Japan: demographic aging in 77, 108–10, 113; employment rates in 132; midlife in 94; pension programs in 102; premodern 40
Jaworska, Angieszka 132
Jews 59, 88, 117, 139

Jiang, Lin 109–10
Johnson, Paul 5
joint family (India) 111, 122
Judaism 26–7, 34, 44
Jullien, François 20
Juvenal 32

Katrina, Hurricane 141
Katz, Stephen 120, 123
Kenya 10, 12
Kerala 110
Kidder, Tracy 136
Kittredge, Katharine 5
Korea 40, 108–9, 113, 122
Kugler, Anne 58
Kuhn, Maggie 141

Lalive d'Epinay, Christian 135–6
Lamb, Sarah 110
Lanza, Janine 49
Laslett, Peter xi, 4, 128, 131
Latin America 77, 87–8, 97, 113–14
Latino aging 138–40
Lee, Ronald 76–7
Lellouch, Alain 118–19
liberalism 82, 84
life expectancy: eighteenth-century 61, 68; in good health 128; increase in contemporary era 110, 120; maximum 129; medieval 46; rates by race 139; Roman 30
life course divided into training/work/retirement 90, 100
life span, ideal 24, 25
Lindenmeyr, Adele 107
Lorcin, Marie-Thérèse 47
Loriaux, Michel 128
Lucca 50
Luce, Judith de 29

maintenance contracts 48, 50–1, 68
Malaysia 109
Mali 91
Malthus, Thomas 74
Marin, Bernd 129–31
Marshall, Alfred 83
Martin, Jean-Pierre 118–19
masculinity 72, 89, 91
McKerlie, Dennis 132
McNally, Michael David 13–14, 140
media, mass 137
medicine 18, 116–22; and anthropology 111; colonial and postcolonial 94; in Islamic world 42; medieval 46; nineteenth-century 73
Mehl, R. 90
Mekranoti 10
memoir 136–7
menopause 25, 30, 33, 44, 94
Mesoamerica 87–8, 116
Mesopotamia 24–5, 44, 116
Metchnikoff, Élie 119
Mexican Americans 138–140
midlife 94, 137
migration 75, 94, 112–13; and Arab medicine 18; and contemporary aging 133–4, 137–42; South Asian 111; sub-Saharan 12
Minois, Georges 26–7, 51, 52
missionaries 87, 89
modernization xii, 4–5, 111
monasticism 19, 47
mortality 12, 75, 128
mothers-in-law: central European 50–1; Japanese 108
Myerhoff, Barbara 136
Mzali, M.S. 90

Na 12
Namibia 111
Napoleon 82
narrative 136
Nascher, I.L. 119
Neolithic 12
Nestor 27
Netherlands 59, 132
New Zealand 84, 96–7
notional-defined-contributions system (NDC) 131
Nuland, Sherwin 111, 136
Nursi, Said 42–4, 127

Obasuteyama 40
old age: festival of 69; "good" 112; historiography of 3–8; as social problem xiv, 78, 81–6
oral histories 92, 136
oral tradition 90–1
Osler, William 121
Ottaway, Susannah 5, 61–2

Papua New Guinea 12
Paraguay 11
Parkin, Tim 28–32
Pasteur Institute 119
Pennock, Caroline Dodds 88

pensions and pensioners xiv; in Africa 91–2; contemporary 129–33; early modern 60; medieval 48; modern 81–6; in welfare state 96–102
Peru 116
Peterson, Peter 136
Philippines 113
philosophy: and aging 59, 117, 131–2; new-age 93; and welfare state 84, 101
Plato 28
Pliny the Elder 31–2
po ocheredi 107
Poland 131
Poor Law, English 60, 61, 83, 97
Posner, Richard 131, 136
poverty: in Africa 112; and African American aging 139; in ancient Greece and Rome 29; early modern 59, 60, 69; immigration and 138; modern 82–3, 84, 120; in pre-Revolutionary Russia 107–8; and welfare state 98
prehistory 11–13
Premo, Terri L. 6
privatization 101, 131
professional journals and societies 122
Protestants 88
psychology and aging 134–6

Quadagno, Jill 6
Quetelet, Adolphe 121
Quran 40–4

race 137–9
Reagan, Ronald 101
rectangular curve 128
Renaissance 34, 51–4, 57, 117
rentes 61
retirement xi; in Africa 112; contemporary 129–34; and European working class 84; medieval 47–8, 52–3; Roman 31; and welfare state 98, 100, 101
retreat 17, 18
Richardson, Bessie 29
Romanticism 70
Rome 16, 29–34
Rosenmayr, Leopold 90, 138
Rosenthal, Joel 47
Rowntree, B. Seebohm 121
Rubinow, I.M. 121
Rudaki 41
Ruggles, Steven 61
Rumi 41

Rush, Benjamin 73, 89
Russia 93, 107–8, 130–1

Sahagún, Bernardino of 88
Salpêtrière 118–20
Samburu 10
Scandinavia 84, 96; see also individual countries
Schaie, K. Warner 123
science xiii, 53–4, 59–60
second childhood 88, 135
Second World War 84, 96, 98, 108
secularization xiii, 43, 62, 70
Seeman, Erik 88
Seltzer, Mildred M. 129
Seneca 16, 31–2
Senegal 91
senicide or "senilicide" 11, 34
seniors 130
sexuality 32, 49, 52, 88, 117, 134, 137
Shahar, Shulamith 44–50
Shakespeare, William 127, 132; *As You Like It* 52; *King Lear* 48, 51
Siena 49–50
Simmons, Leo 9–10, 12
Sinclair, Upton 98
Singapore 108–9, 113
Sivaramakrishnan, Kavita 122
slaves 88, 89
Slovakia 131
Small, Helen 132
social class 71, 134
social rights 84–5
social sciences 121
Social Security (US) 98–9
social surveys 121
sociology and aging xii, 90, 100, 124–5, 132–6
Socrates 16
Sokoll, Thomas 61
Sophocles, *Oedipus at Colonus* 28–9
South Africa 84, 91–2, 111–12
Spencer, Paul 10
Sprockhoff, Joachim 18
Stahl, Georg Ernst 117
Stahmer, Harold M. 26
state xiii, 60, 157
Stearns, Peter xii, 5, 12–13, 119
Stewart, Joan Hinde 67
Sundiata 90
Sweden 77, 84, 99, 131, 132, 140
Switzerland 135–6

Taiwan 108–9, 113
Tajikistan 108
Terkel, Studs 136
Thailand 19
Thane, Pat 5, 6, 61, 82, 101
Thatcher, Margaret 101
third age (or young old) 24, 129, 132, 142; universities of 4
Thomson, David 82, 101
tontines 61
Torres-Gil, Fernando M. 140
Townsend Plan 98
Trollope, Anthony, "The Fixed Period" 121
Troyansky, David G. 5, 46, 58, 62, 67–9, 82
Tubiana, Maurice 136
Tunisia 92–3, 113
Turkey, 42–4
Turkmenistan 108
Tuscany 49

Uganda 112–13
Unani 18, 93
United States: demographic transition in 75–7; geriatrics in 119; historiography of old age in 4–6; nineteenth-century 71–2; pensions in 81, 84; social security era in 98, 102
Upanishads 17
Uruguay 113

Vaughan, Megan 112
Veda 17, 18
Venice 50
vital revolution 76

welfare state 85, 96–103, 107
Werner, Dennis 10
West: and idealization of Asian aging 18; as norm xii-xiii, 107, 114, 122
Wezler, Albrecht 18
widowhood 25, 34, 49
Williams, Alun 112–13
Williams, Bernard 131
witches 46, 58–9
women and aging: in Africa 92, 111, 113; in African American history 89; anthropology of 9–11; historiography of 6; in Mesopotamia 24–5; in Middle Ages and Renaissance 42, 46, 47, 52, 53
women and work 108, 130
women's pensions 85
workforce 98; participation in England 99–100
workhouses 60–1
World Bank 113, 142
World Health Organization 127

Zahan, Dominique 90
Zambia 112
Zulu 12
Zysk, Kenneth 18